REIKI

HAWAYO TAKATA'S STORY

REIKI

HAWAYO TAKATA'S STORY

By

Helen J. Haberly

ARCHEDIGM®

Reiki: Hawayo Takata's Story

7th printing .... April 1996

Published by Archedigm Publications
Division of Archedigm, Inc.
P.O. Box 1109
Olney, MD 20830–1109

Cover Design: Arts & Letters, Ltd.
Typesetting: Sans Serif, Inc.
McNaughton & Gunn, Inc., Lithographers

Manufactured in the U.S.A.

ISBN 0–944135–06–04

Dedicated

to

The Memory Of

HAWAYO K. TAKATA

my Teacher

my Friend

Acknowledgments

This is a story—not a history—as Hawayo Takata told it; and as with any life story, there are countless individuals who have added their chapters and paragraphs, most of whom will remain here unnamed. To those whose interviews substantiated the facts upon which the story is told, I give my heartfelt "thank you." Your generous sharing of personal experiences with Mrs. Takata and with Reiki have added much enrichment.

I give special thanks to those in my life who have helped make this work possible:

My daughters and sons, their mates and children, who have been my strong supporters and who share their Reiki with me.

Louis, who introduced me to Hawayo Takata and Reiki.

The late Reiki Master Bethal Phaigh, with her unwavering faith in my promise to write this story.

Reiki Master Lani Kaito, whose unique insights helped give form and focus to the writing.

Dr. Carroll F. Raaum, for his literary criticism and continuing support in my life journey.

Grand Master, Phyllis Lei Furumoto, for use of family pictures.

Walter R. Jackson, photographer and friend, for his generous contribution of time and advice.

Mavis McLaverty, for her magic with the computer.

Reiki Master Linda Keiser Mardis, sister in spirit, and her partner, Arthur Mardis, who together bring the energy and knowledge needed to manifest such a book.

REIKI

HAWAYO TAKATA'S STORY

Hawayo K. Takata
1900 - 1980
Photograph by Günter Baylow

Introduction

For forty-five years Hawayo Takata carried in her hands—literally—one of the world's great healing arts which she called Reiki. She shared this knowledge with hundreds of students and treated thousands of sufferers during her long career as teacher and practitioner of Reiki.

Her path and mine converged in the early fall of 1973 when she traveled from her island home in Hawaii to teach a class on another island, this one off the Northwest coast of the state of Washington. I was one of thirty students in that class, and when this small Oriental woman stood before us and said firmly, "Reiki means Universal Life Energy and we are all composed of this energy. *Everyone* can use this energy for healing — and I can teach you how!" I knew she had the answers for which I had been searching.

This had been a long and diligent quest of more than seventeen years, one motivated by my need to understand more fully what had occurred in my life with a profound spiritual experience, a transformational event which even now I can describe inadequately only as "mystical."

My conventional Christian rearing had not prepared me to comprehend nor cope with the energy which was spontaneously released as a result of this experience, and I found little comfort or help within the structure of my church. Instead, books began to gravitate to me and in the writings of the mystics, ancient and contemporary, I found validation for what had happened. The teachings of Jesus took on new depth and meaning in my life, and the way was opened for me to seek more answers in the study of the world's great religions—in theology—philosophy—psychology—parapsychology — and in science, especially the "new physics."

I read the popular literature on healing and healers and attended workshops and lectures on this subject. I sat in meetings with some of the world's renowned spiritual healers, and I learned much about healing; yet no one seemed able to give me direction or assistance in utilizing my own abilities until Mrs. Takata stated clearly that September evening, ". . . I can teach you how!" — and she did. With my Reiki training, the search was completed; and this became the pivotal moment when my life began to change beyond imagining.

In her visits to the Pacific Northwest I came to know Hawayo Takata both as teacher and as friend, and when in 1980 she asked me to write her life story with Reiki, I was honored to do so. Before the manuscript was completed she made her transition, and the project was put aside temporarily, although I knew at the appropriate time my promise to her would be fulfilled.

In addition to those Masters initiated by Mrs. Takata, in the past eight years many more have been trained to carry on this work and I am privileged to be among them. To the Masters and to the thousands of students who now carry Reiki to the world, I offer this gift from Grand Master Hawayo K. Takata.

Helen J. Haberly

CHAPTER ONE

Once upon a time—for all proper stories begin with "Once upon a time" —a gift of great value was given to the Children of Earth. Not all people recognized it as a great gift nor honored it as such, but it was, nonetheless, a wondrous offering to those who could understand and accept what had been given.

Throughout the ages there have been stories of this magical gift which came to be called "healing." It has been talked of in many times and in many places—in such ancient lands as Egypt and Tibet and China—and in other countries past remembering. Some said it was just a myth without substance—others declared it was so. Many such stories grew around the activities of great Teachers who had come to Earth—the Avatars—for it was said that each of them had brought this gift of healing when they had come to share their messages of Truth with the Children of Earth; yet such magic was no longer known nor practiced, and there were few, if any, who could truly say such a thing had ever existed.

There were many legends about the healing miracles of these great Teachers, but such stories were easily dismissed when there had been no demonstrations of it for hundreds of years—if, indeed, such events had *ever* occurred. Those who insisted upon "proof" found none, so the ones who believed that such things were possible held this quietly to themselves, knowing there was no way to prove what they believed.

Into this 19th Century world of skepticism was born in Japan a child who was named Mikao Usui, a boy destined to become a scholar/philosopher, as well as a profound healer. Educated by missionaries, he became a Christian and eventually rose to a position of eminence as head of a Christian boys' school in Kyoto. In his dual role of Minister and Principal, Dr. Usui worked among his students until one morning at Chapel service several of the senior students politely questioned him during the service, asking if he believed the Bible, *literally* believed. When Dr. Usui replied that he did, they then wanted him to demonstrate his belief by performing a miracle, one such as Jesus had done. As Dr. Usui was unable to do this, his students declared his to be a blind faith and insufficient to bolster their own, for they needed more than blind faith in order to believe.

Dr. Usui was struck with the enormity of this questioning and asked the young men not to lose their faith. He declared his intention to immediately resign his position and travel to a Christian country of the West where he would learn how to do the miracles of Jesus, returning then to Kyoto to give literal proof of his beliefs.

America was his destination where he enrolled in a Chicago university to study more deeply the Christian scriptures. His interest was centered on the healing miracles, and when it became apparent that he could not learn from his studies how Jesus healed, he began to delve into the sacred writings of the other great world religions. Eventually he concentrated on the Buddhist writings, having learned that Buddha and his early disciples had performed healing. Intuitively, he sensed that the answer he wanted would be found in this tradition.

After seven years in America, Dr. Usui decided to return to Kyoto where he would be able to study more fully the Buddhist Sutras. There he visited many temples and monasteries, talking with the monks about healing. They were in agreement that Buddha had healed; however, this practice had been dropped from Buddhism, with the monks concerning themselves only with spiritual health and leaving the physical healing to the doctors.

In the course of his search, Dr. Usui met a Zen abbot who invited him to remain in his monastery while pursuing these studies. The invitation was accepted and for several years Dr. Usui remained with these monks. He studied first the writings in Japanese, and not finding what he sought, he decided perhaps much had been lost in the translations. Since Buddhism had been brought to Japan from China, he then learned Chinese and read the Sutras in that language. He knew he was closer but still did not find exactly what he wanted. Again, he questioned the translation, deciding to learn Sanskrit since Buddhism had come originally from India. He became a Sanskrit Master, and it was in this language that Dr. Usui finally found what he had been seeking. The secrets of healing were his! He had found the symbols—yet he did not know what to do with them nor how to use them.

Not willing to accept this as the final answer, he decided to go a few miles outside Kyoto to a mountain considered sacred by the monks, there to fast and meditate for three weeks in the expectation that he would be shown the meaning of the information he had found. He discussed his intention with the abbot, with the request that if he did not return on the twenty-first day some monks be sent to the mountain on the next day to collect his bones. He did not intend to return without an answer.

Dr. Usui walked to this mountain, some seventeen miles from the city, and found a quiet place near a stream where he sat in meditation, allowing himself only water during the long fast. To keep track of the days, he placed beside him a pile of twenty-one small stones, discarding one each day until only one remained.

Thus, in the very early morning of the last day, he sat in the darkness which preceded the dawn, looking into the heavens where he saw a distant light in the black sky. As he watched, this light became very bright and appeared to rush toward him. Nearer and nearer it sped, and he realized it would strike him if he continued to sit there. His first impulse was to dodge. Then he thought of the years he had searched for an answer. So he sat motionless, determined to allow this experience. The light struck him in the forehead and he lost consciousness.

When he came into awareness again the sun was high in the sky, shining brightly, and he knew several hours had passed—yet he had total recall of everything that had occurred during this period of time. When the light struck him he became aware of beautiful colors, one after the other, all the hues of the rainbow. This was followed by an intense white light, after which large transparent bubbles appeared before his eyes, each containing one of the symbols he had found in the Sanskrit writings. As a bubble would move into his field of vision and pause, the instruction in the use of this symbol would be given. As soon as he had committed the information to memory, the bubble would move away and another would replace it with a different symbol. In this fashion Dr. Usui was given the full teachings in the meaning of the symbols. He now had the secrets for which he had searched. He knew this was the Universal Life Energy, which he called "Reiki," and thus was born the Usui System of Natural Healing.

Full of energy and eager to return to Kyoto, Dr. Usui arose from his long meditation and strode down the mountain. As he rushed along, he stubbed his toe quite painfully, so he immediately put to the test what he had learned. As he grasped his toe, he experienced an instant healing and received the first validation of the truth of his vision.

As he continued down the mountain he realized he was very hungry, so coming to a roadside food stand, he seated himself at the table which was covered with a red cloth—the indication that it was open for business. An old man came from the nearby kitchen to take the order. Seeing Dr. Usui's beard and dusty robe, he assumed this meant a long meditation up on the mountain and he was reluctant to bring his guest the usual meal. Instead, he wanted to cook some rice gruel, knowing that after a long fast the stomach needed a gentle introduction back into solid food. Dr. Usui did not want to wait, so insisting on having whatever was already available, he was served pickled vegetables and rice from which he suffered no ill effects.

The meal was brought by the old man's granddaughter, who was in much pain from an infected tooth. Her face was swollen and she had tied a cloth around it, so Dr. Usui asked permission to touch her cheek. The pain immediately ceased and the swelling went down, prompting her and her grandfather to agree this was a most unusual monk. Dr. Usui was elated to have another indication of the truth of his instruction as he proceeded toward Kyoto.

The monks greeted him with gladness, pleased he had returned on the twenty-first day alive and healthy. Inquiring after the head of the monastery, he learned that the abbot was in his quarters suffering great pain from arthritis; so as soon as he had bathed and dressed in clean robes, Dr. Usui went to make his report. The abbot was very happy to hear that the search of long years had been rewarded and the secrets of healing had been revealed. He asked for a demonstration which immediately relieved his pain.

The two men discussed what should be done with this great knowledge, and Dr. Usui decided to go into the vast slums of Kyoto where he would offer healing to the beggars. He would then send the younger ones to the monastery where they would be trained by the monks in skills which would help them earn their living.

In those days the slums were an unsafe place for strangers to enter, for the beggars banded together under a leader and they did not welcome others among them. Dr. Usui sought out the Chief of the beggars, asking permission to live there and heal the people, his only requirements being a place to sleep and to do his work, along with three bowls of rice a day. His request was granted, so he moved into this area and started the healing work among these poor people, a task that fully occupied his time for a number of years.

Eventually, he began to notice familiar faces as he walked about the neighborhood, and upon inquiry, learned that these were indeed some of the young people he had healed and sent to the monastery for training. They had returned to the slums because they found earning a living to be much harder than going out to beg each day.

Upon hearing this, Dr. Usui felt himself to be a great failure, so he left the slums immediately. Withdrawing to meditate upon what had happened, he remembered his early discussions with the monks in which they spoke of their deep concern with the spiritual healing of their followers. He realized that although he had been very successful in balancing the physical bodies of the beggars, he had had no concern for their spiritual health. At this time he added to Reiki his Five Spiritual Precepts:

Just for today, do not worry.
Just for today, do not anger.
Honor your teachers, your parents,
your neighbors, your friends.
Give thanks for all living things.
Earn your living honestly.

Dr. Usui also realized that in his giving away Reiki so freely, the beggars had developed no appreciation for it; they had no gratitude for this wonderful gift which had been given through him. He determined never again to give Reiki to anyone who did not appreciate it.

He began to travel throughout Japan from town to town, teaching others about Reiki. He was a wise and clever teacher, so having arrived in a town where he knew no one, he would walk through the market place in the daytime, carrying a lighted torch. The people would laugh and make fun of such a silly man, carrying a torch when the sun was shining. Thus capturing their attention, Dr. Usui would invite them to attend his meeting that evening if they really wanted to learn about light. In this way he gathered the people to hear the story of Reiki, after which many wanted to learn how to do this healing.

He developed a large following of students and in the mid-1920's he met a man who became his most dedicated disciple, Dr. Chujiro Hayashi, a forty-seven year old Reserve Naval Officer. With the transition of Dr. Usui, Dr. Hayashi became the Reiki Grand Master, carrying on this tradition of teaching and healing from his clinic in Tokyo.

Dr. Hayashi was from an illustrious family whose country home was in Atami. When he decided to open a clinic, Tokyo was chosen as the location, which allowed Reiki to be offered to a larger group of people and attracted the affluent and educated, even a high ranking segment of Japanese society, the nobility. In one generation, Reiki had leaped from the slums of Kyoto to the palaces of Tokyo.

He acquired a property large enough to accommodate both the clinic and a home for his family, with a beautiful garden between the two areas to provide privacy. Mrs. Hayashi also worked in the clinic, greeting the patients as they arrived and assisting Dr. Hayashi as he supervised this thriving practice where daily sixteen practitioners gave Reiki treatments.

It was to this clinic that a young woman named Hawayo Takata came in the Fall of 1935, seeking relief from her multiple ailments; and no one recognized in her the future Grand Master of Reiki.

CHAPTER TWO

The story of Hawayo Takata began in 1900, early in the morning of Christmas Eve when she was born at Hanamaulu on the island of Kauai, Hawaii. As was the custom of the immigrants from Japan in the late 1800's, her parents sought the services of the midwife for this occasion, so when the mother asked the time of birth, the response was it was dawn and the sun was just coming over the hill. The mother then requested that the baby be bathed, wrapped in a new blanket, and held by the midwife to face the sun while naming the child "Hawayo" in honor of the newly formed Territory of Hawaii.

Hawayo's father worked in the sugar cane fields of the nearby plantation, and life in this village was very simple with much hard labor. She attended public school, as did all the village children, a pleasure for her since she enjoyed learning.

When she was twelve years old she joined the other students who went to the plantation fields to work during the summer, cutting the cane seedlings. The cane cutters would go out into the large fields to cut down the tall stalks with sharp knives. Then the children would lop off the tops, filling gunny sacks with these short pieces of cane. Hawayo went to the fields with the others and she worked diligently, but it was very difficult for her because she was quite small and delicate.

She did her best to fill the bag, but when the supervisor shook it, it was only three-fourths full and she had to fill it to the top again. She saw her companions getting farther and farther ahead, and afraid of being left alone, she began to cry. Two family friends who were cutting cane nearby saw her distress and offered to help her, using part of their lunch hour to fill her bags completely. This continued all summer and, with the help of her friends, she was able to keep up with her schoolmates.

On the last day when the work was ended, the other children clambered aboard the cane car behind the locomotive waiting to take them home, but Hawayo sat down on the ground and lifted her hands heavenward to offer up her petition that she never have to do this work again, saying, "God, please let me do better things with my hands and do not send me back to the cane field again, forever and ever." Little did she realize that her prayer would be granted fully twenty-five years later with Reiki; but somehow year after year when her friends went back to the fields to earn their summer money, she had other jobs and never returned to the cane field.

This scene in the field was observed and taken to heart by the locomotive engineer who came one day to talk about it with Hawayo's father. He told of the difficulties she had had and how their friends had helped fill the bags. Her father had not known she was having problems in the fields, but he understood that she was not going to be a good worker there because of her small size; so when the principal of the church boarding school asked if she might live in his home and assist with teaching the first grade, deep consideration was given to this request. Assured that she could complete her education by doing her own grade work at night, permission was given for her to go. Every Friday when she returned home for the weekend she gave her wages to her parents—a five dollar gold piece and a silver dollar—which was a very great help to her family.

In 1914 she attended the opening of a store in Lihue some twenty miles from her home. This was an unusual event, with many people coming to see the new store, so business was active that day. The man who was in charge of the soda fountain knew Hawayo and asked if she could lend a hand since he was overworked, so she agreed to wash the dishes and help serve the customers. When the store closed that evening, he drove her home in his buggy and spoke with her parents, saying he was in need of a helper and would they allow Hawayo to have that job. Again, deep thought was given, and it was agreed that she could help him on Saturdays. Thus she had two jobs while still a student, and when she finished public school, she automatically had a full-time job at the store.

She continued to live at the boarding school where she attended Japanese school from six to eight in the morning and then walked seven miles to work. After a time the manager asked her to come into the office and file papers during her spare time at the soda fountain, so with two jobs, there was never a dull moment—and very few for relaxation.

One day there came to the store a very elegant lady, the daughter of a wealthy plantation owner, who took notice of the girl because she was pleased with the service given; and she soon offered Hawayo a job, promising to supply room and board, clothing, and double the salary earned at the store. Since she already had a good job, and this involved a major move, it was a difficult decision. Finally she accepted the lady's invitation to visit during vacation.

She had never seen such an estate—a beautiful mansion, five cottages, and a big stable, as well as other outbuildings needed for the plantation. She was introduced to the cook who urged her to stay, saying the work was not hard, the pay was good, and she would be dressed very beautifully in kimono and obi. Her parents, too, readily agreed since she would no longer live so far away at the boarding school, making it possible to visit them every weekend. She decided to ask the store manager to release her with a recommendation so if she failed in her new job, she could go back to the old one.

Thus began her association with this lady, one which was to continue for twenty-four years. Starting as a waitress-pantry girl, eventually she was promoted to Number One Housekeeper, and because she had experience with bookkeeping at the store, she began to handle the paychecks as well as supervise the twenty-one staff members.

When she began working in this home, the plantation company's bookkeeper was Saichi Takata, a young man to whom she was introduced and, in time, married. This was a happy marriage, made even more so with the births of two daughters.

Although busy with their employment and family, there was still time for Saichi to serve on the Welfare Board of the district, the first person of Oriental descent to be appointed to such a position by the Territorial Governor, and he took pride in this assignment. He helped with service clubs and sports activities, for he was a baseball fan and pitcher himself. His life was full and they did not realize how short it was to be.

One October morning in 1930 while still at the breakfast table he spoke to Hawayo of his views on life and death, expressing his understanding that to everything that is born there will come a time of change which he called transition; that everything goes through this great change, but there is in truth no death; and in the human life when this time comes, no one can stop it. He instructed her, should he go into transition first, not to be shocked nor to grieve, but instead, to look up and smile for then he would know that she also understood the laws of nature. He told her how he wanted his memorial meal to be arranged, leaving one chair open, for he would be there. He also told her not to bury him in Hawaii. He did not want a grave, for she would be attached to that place.

She did not want to accept what he said and declared her need for his help at her side, teaching her and giving guidance and courage. He assured her this would be possible in any case, for nothing is impossible, and he knew she would try very hard even if he were not with her. It was difficult to believe any of this would happen, but on the third day after this conversation, Saichi made his transition very suddenly at the young age of thirty-four. This was a great shock and loss not only to Hawayo and the family, but also to the community; and although everything was done according to his wishes, she was very sad and missed him greatly.

CHAPTER THREE

After her husband's transition she kept her word and worked very hard to provide the financial care for her family. From 1930 to 1935 she had little rest and finally suffered a nervous breakdown from overwork. In addition, she had severe physical problems—a painful abdominal condition which required surgery and respiratory problems which prevented the use of the anesthetic. The doctor informed her she must have the surgery if she was to live, and since it appeared she would not survive the operation, he felt he could not accept responsibility for it.

She was in a desperate situation and knew she was losing ground, so at night when her chores were completed, she would sit under the big camphor tree where she sought peace of mind in meditation. She was not yet thirty-five years old, but she felt sixty, for she was unable to walk upright because of the pain in her abdomen. At times she had great difficulty breathing. She looked into the heavens and prayed for guidance, not knowing which way to turn.

One such night when it was so dark there was not even a star in sight, she heard very clearly a voice from above telling her she would have even more problems, and the first thing for her to do was to recover her health, for only then would she be able to work and earn, thus assuring security and long life. She bowed her head to the earth in thankfulness and accepted this message, asking to be shown the way to accomplish it.

Within three weeks one of her sisters died very suddenly after a four-day illness. It was a very sorrowful moment in Hawayo's life for it was her duty to deliver this sad news to her parents who were in Japan at this time, having returned for a one-year stay in their family home at Yamaguchi, her father's first visit since his immigration to Hawaii forty years previously.

To have written this news in a letter would have been too great a shock, so she decided to go to Japan personally to see them and to seek also some relief for her poor state of health. Accompanied by her sister-in-law, she set forth on the steamship.

For five years she had waited for some means of taking her husband's ashes to Kyoto for a service at the Ohtani Temple, so she carried them with her. Aboard ship she met a Buddhist minister from Kona, Hawaii, who would be in residence at this large temple, and he offered his assistance by taking charge of the urn, carrying it to Kyoto while she went to Yamaguchi, with the understanding she would meet him at the Ohtani Temple in six months, March of 1936. This would allow time for her to go to her parents and afterward enter a Tokyo hospital for treatment to improve her health.

After the services for her sister, she went to Tokyo and entered a small private hospital in Akasaka. The surgeon agreed her body needed much attention, but decided against an immediate operation. Instead, he urged her to think of this place not as a hospital, but a resort where she was to rest and eat well, and when she had gained some weight they would consider what was to be done.

It was three weeks before he called her in for a thorough examination, and he confirmed she had a tumor, gallstones, and appendicitis, these being the cause of her abdominal pain. He then scheduled her surgery at seven A.M. the next day.

Early in the morning she was taken to the operating room where her body was prepared for the surgery. The nurses were arranging the sterilized instruments, the gauze, and the equipment, while the doctors were at the sink scrubbing their hands. Mrs. Takata was lying very still on the surgical table, eyes closed, listening to the splashing of the water and the conversations, when suddenly she heard quite clearly a voice saying, "The operation is not necessary. The operation is not necessary." She opened her eyes and looked around but saw no one speaking. She pinched herself to make sure she was not dreaming, and she decided if she heard the voice the third time, she would accept it. It was even louder the third time, "The operation is not necessary!" She knew she was awake and sane, but what could she do? The voice said, "Ask . . . ask . . . ask." Whom should she ask? "The head surgeon . . . the head surgeon . . . the head surgeon."

She slipped off the table and stood on the floor, sheet wrapped around her. The nurses rushed over and began to scold her for spoiling their preparations for the surgery. The doctors also came, with the surgeon expressing concern that she might be reacting from fear of the operation. She assured him this was not so, that she was not afraid, not even nervous, but she had a question for him. Did he know of any other treatment or therapy that would help her? He thought a few moments and said he did, but it would depend upon how much time she was willing to spend in Tokyo. There was no way to know how long this treatment might take—two weeks, two months, or a year—and likely it would not work if she had come for both a cure and a tour of Japan in sixty days. Because he had said a year, she doubled it, declaring she could stay two years, since health was her first concern, not sightseeing.

The doctor sent for his sister, who was also the hospital dietitian, and she took Mrs. Takata by streetcar to another section of the city to a studio where drugless treatment was given. They were welcomed by Mrs. Hayashi, the director's wife, who also served as the receptionist; and when Mrs. Takata's turn came, she entered the treatment room where she saw eight couches with sixteen men practitioners giving treatments under the supervision of Dr. Chujiro Hayashi.

Fully clothed, she lay down upon a couch and two

practitioners began the treatment, one man working on her head, the other on her abdomen. As their hands lightly touched her, they would comment on what they were sensing: "Oh, yes, your gall bladder is not too good; you must have a lot of pain here," and "There is a lump here; it could be a tumor," and so on. When they made such observations she could feel the heat from their hands, but she did not understand how they knew these things and wondered if the hospital had called them. How did they know? She was very curious but decided to save her questions for the next day when she would return at an earlier hour to allow time for such inquiries.

The next day the doctor's sister again went with her to the clinic, but before Mrs. Takata lay down on the couch she looked under it to see if there were wiring connections to some sort of instrument or battery that created the heat. Then she looked at the ceiling to see if there were any wires from above, and in both cases there were none. Therefore, she assumed, the practitioners must have instruments in their pockets, so she decided to test them.

As the treatment began, she reached up and grabbed the sleeve of the man treating her right side. Startled by this, he took a tissue from his kimono and offered it to her; but she declined politely, saying she was interested in his pocket because she thought he had some sort of machine there. He began to laugh and shook his sleeves so she could see they were empty, while Dr. Hayashi came to see what was happening. She voiced her curiosity, wondering how the practitioner could tell where she had pain and what was amiss, saying, "I know his hands are giving him the message, for they are hot and I can feel the vibration. They are no ordinary hands, so he must have a connection with some kind of power."

"Yes," Dr. Hayashi replied, "He does, but it is not electricity. This is Reiki." She asked him to explain more fully since she was not completely familiar with the language. "Reiki is the Japanese word for Universal Life Energy. In English it sounds like 'Ray-key,' and it comes from space, from the universe. The only thing that is different between you and us is that we have the contact with the Universal Life Force and you do not. My practitioners all have this contact and they can use it. They are applying it now and are filling your body with Life Energy. This is so big we cannot measure it, so deep we cannot fathom it; therefore, in Japanese we call it Reiki."

She thanked him, although she understood little of what he had said. He continued, "Do you have radio in Hawaii? When the radio station broadcasts, there are no lines connected from the station to your house, yet as you turn on the receiver and contact the station, you receive what they are sending. Because we are not radio technicians, we do not know how. The principles are the same with Reiki. This energy goes through space without wires, and we know this great force can be contacted. Once the contact is made, the energy flow is automatic. It is universal, limitless energy. When you have the switch on, the power is unlimited. When you want to stop, you just take your hands away. It is very simple."

On the way back to the hospital Mrs. Takata's companion, the doctor's sister, told her that in Japan the women were silent and refrained from expressing themselves and displaying emotions in public. However, Dr. Hayashi had explained to his practitioners that although Mrs. Takata looked Japanese and had a Japanese name, she was an American and her questions were proper for a Western woman, not strange or rude. She then requested that Mrs. Takata not ask any more questions at the clinic, but to save them until they returned home and she would answer them. She offered to come to Mrs. Takata's room after her day's work and give a treatment, and while that was going on, they could discuss Reiki. Mrs. Takata was amazed to learn that this lady had taken the lessons and could also do this Reiki.

That evening she gave Mrs. Takata a complete treatment and confirmed what the practitioners had said, stating, "Yes, what they told you is correct. I find the same vibrations. Everyone diagnoses the same because the vibrations are the same. You are the one putting forth these vibrations and we feel it in our hands." Mrs. Takata wanted to know why she had taken this training since she worked at a hospital, and the lady told her story. She had had severe dysentery and was near death in a coma. Her daughter, away at school, was getting ready to come to the hospital when a classmate asked her to go first to Dr. Hayashi and to seek his assistance. Hearing about her mother, he agreed to go to the hospital where he treated her and with that one Reiki treatment, she regained consciousness. He continued to treat her until she recovered. When she was strong enough, she took the training, offering her assistance in her brother's hospital whenever patients did not want drugs or pain killers. She also used the Reiki to help in the food preparation, for as the dietitian, she would touch the food and vitalize it, filling it with Life Energy to benefit the patients.

When she heard this story, Mrs. Takata became very interested in learning to do Reiki, also, but the doctor's sister gave her no encouragement, saying that Japan had given many, many cultures to the outside world—kendo, judo, karate, tea ceremony, flower arrangement—but not Reiki. It was being carefully guarded and was not to leave Japan. This was difficult for Mrs. Takata to accept, as she felt she had just discovered hope for life with Reiki; but if that was the rule, she would say no more. She was determined, however, to find a way.

Although she went daily to Dr. Hayashi's clinic for a treatment, she still stayed in the hospital. Here she began her meditations, praying for guidance for a way to gain entrance into the Reiki classes. She had come this far to find the answer to her health problems, and having found it, she could not believe the door was closed to her. Finally, it occurred to her to ask the help of the surgeon.

After three weeks of Reiki treatments, the doctor met her in the hall one day and inquired about her progress. He was very pleased to see how well she looked, commenting she was on the way to recovery and to keep up the good work. Here was her opportunity, so taking courage, she asked him to help her in her desire to take the training. He responded that there were rules and there was etiquette, and he could do nothing since this association did not want to accept outsiders.

She pressed her case, saying she could not come to Japan every time she needed a treatment and that she wanted to learn Reiki in order to stand on her own and support herself and her family. With this plea, he said he would try to help, although he could promise nothing.

He wrote to Dr. Hayashi, putting forth her request, and this was no ordinary letter. Instead, the doctor took a long scroll and wrote it himself with his brush and ink. He instructed his sister to deliver this letter into the hands of Mrs. Hayashi. When it was given to Dr. Hayashi by his wife, he was very impressed, saying he was highly honored to receive such a letter, handwritten by this great surgeon. Dr. Hayashi called the directors of the association to a meeting where this appeal was read. It was decided to allow Mrs. Takata to become an honorary member, a special privilege which would permit her to take the Reiki lessons; and when the next class was offered, she was allowed to enroll.

Along with the other students, she was empowered by Dr. Hayashi to receive the Universal Life Energy, to make the contact with this limitless force. He told them this contact would be made in four small steps called "initiations," and four days would be required to complete the First Degree of Reiki.

During the lessons he explained the treatment, the first day dealing with the body above the neck—the head, eyes, ears, nose, and throat—and the conditions and diseases which would be found in these areas. On the second day they were taught how to treat the front of the body, the chest and abdomen, with all the organs located here. The lesson for the third day dealt with the back, which included the spine, nerve systems, and organs. They were shown where and how to place their hands to permit the Life Energy to flow to the body of the patient, allowing Reiki to balance the condition or ailment so healing could occur.

On the fourth day Dr. Hayashi discussed how to heal in acute cases, such as accidents. He also spoke of the spiritual side of Reiki, for which were given the Five Ideals:

> Just for today, do not anger.
> Just for today, do not worry.
> Honor your teachers, your father
> and mother, and your neighbors;

count your blessings; and show
appreciation for your food.
Earn your living honestly.
Be kind to everything that has life.

They were taught there is always the cause and effect: remove the cause and there shall be no effect. Reiki will work as long as the practitioner believes it, applies it, and continues to use it.

In her own case she knew Reiki to be a powerful healing energy. After just three weeks of daily treatments, she was much better. Her body had rid itself of its toxins, all the aches and pains had disappeared, her color was better than it had ever been, and her strength was returning. She felt light as a feather and could move easily. By the end of four months her respiratory problems were gone, and the gallstones had come out. She was so well by this time that she felt she should practice the Reiki she had learned in the class.

When six months had passed, she went to Kyoto as planned where the services were held for her husband. It was time, also, for her parents to return to Hawaii, so after seeing them off on the steamship, she moved to the Hayashi home, accepting their invitation to live with them while she learned to be a Reiki practitioner.

When the first patients started arriving at seven each morning, Mrs. Takata was in the clinic with the other sixteen practitioners, where for five hours there was not an idle moment. The afternoons were used for house calls, sometimes requiring a train ride of two or three hours out into the country and back again after treating the patient. Following her evening meal she gave the report of her afternoon's activities to Dr. Hayashi and his family. This was her daily routine for one year, with every day devoted to the practice of Reiki.

At times Dr. Hayashi took her with him on house calls into very lovely private homes, some belonging to titled people. One of her memorable experiences was a visit with Dr. Hayashi to an Archbishop of the Jodo Mission Sect (Buddhist) in Kamakura who, having severe laryngitis, had lost his voice for several years. No longer able to perform the duties of his office, he was forced into early retirement. After his fourth Reiki treatment he experienced a reaction in which his throat rid itself of this toxic condition, and he began to recover rapidly. Dr. Hayashi was pleased, saying total recovery could be expected within twenty-one days, and he gave the case over to Mrs. Takata. With the return of his voice, the Archbishop was reinstated and sent to Hawaii to head the work of this group there, as well as on the American mainland. She met him later in Honolulu, where he often invited her to breakfast after the early morning service.

During this year she worked very long hours, with no time to visit shops or call on friends, for everything was for Reiki. She observed what kind of patients came, how well they responded, how long their treatments took. She soon learned that with every condition, it was as Dr. Hayashi had taught: "Remove the cause and there shall be no effect."

At the end of her training she was surprised to learn that every move she had made during that year had been noted, so she was happy that she had done the proper thing and now was allowed the privilege of receiving the Second Degree in Reiki, the Practitioner's Level.

Before she left Tokyo she asked Dr. Hayashi one question which had been bothering her. In all those months at the clinic she had never encountered one poor person—no shabby patients, no laborers—so she asked if he refused to treat such people. He laughed, replying since this was a very good question, he would answer it. He told her that all those who entered his door were upper class, even titled, people of wealth, education, and intelligence. When they were ill they could afford the best doctors and the best hospitals, but they sought more than surgery and drugs. They had Reiki consciousness, so they came to him. The others did not have this understanding, and when illness occurred they thought the need was for hospitals and doctors and nurses. If called, he would go, no matter how poor they were, but their beliefs were different, so they did not accept him and this drugless treatment. He also assured her when she became an experienced practitioner, she, too, would find this to be so.

Mikao Usui

Chujiro Hayashi

Hawayo Takata and Chujiro Hayashi
C. 1938

CHAPTER FOUR

Having completed her training with Dr. Hayashi, Mrs. Takata returned home to Kauai in the summer of 1937. A few weeks later Dr. Hayashi and his daughter arrived to spend six months visiting and helping establish Reiki in Hawaii. It was decided that Honolulu would be the best place to offer classes, so they rented two hotel bungalows and began offering free lectures and demonstrations of this healing art. The editor of the Japanese newspaper was very helpful, publishing pictures and articles in support of Reiki, so within a short time it was well received by the people. Soon they rented a larger hall where lectures and classes were given by Dr. Hayashi, with Mrs. Takata assisting.

In February, 1938, when it was time for Dr. Hayashi to return to Tokyo, his friends gave a banquet in his honor, where they presented him with many gifts and mementos of his visit to Hawaii, expressions of gratitude for allowing Reiki to be taken beyond Japan. He used this occasion to announce publicly that Mrs. Takata was a Reiki Master, chosen for this work because she had gone through many tests and had lived up to the Reiki Ideals and Principles; so it was widely known that she was qualified to continue the Reiki practice and to teach classes in Hawaii. At this time the Archbishop of the Jodo Mission was planning his first trip to the American mainland to visit the churches and meet the ministers in California. None of the twelve members in his entourage spoke English, so he asked Mrs. Takata to join them as their interpreter. She felt this was an honor and, also needing a vacation, she accepted the invitation.

She traveled extensively along the West Coast with these ministers and when the tour was over, she continued on to Chicago, entering the National College of Drugless Physicians to study various therapies, as well as anatomy. When she completed her studies in July, 1938, she returned to Honolulu with confidence, knowing much more about the physical and technical side of the human body. She thought back to that October morning almost three years previously when she had gone to Dr. Hayashi's clinic for her first treatment, and it seemed a miracle that she was now ready to begin her own Reiki practice.

In late December of that year she was invited to make a presentation of Reiki at Kamuela (Waimea), her first visit to the Big Island of Hawaii. Kamuela was one of the larger towns on this island, and some of the citizens of that community were waiting for introductions at the home of her host and hostess. They were not convinced of the value of what she was teaching, so they informed her that Reiki would have to be proven here and gave her two weeks to work on two patients. The first had a chronic heart condition which prevented any physical activity; and the other had acute tonsillitis, with surgery planned when he was stronger. It was a great challenge, but these people said they were willing to learn Reiki if the two showed good results with the treatments.

Both patients responded quickly to the healing energy, and at the end of the allotted time, the woman with the heart condition was able to be up and about, visiting with her friends, and walking to the store to shop. The man had experienced a reaction which released the toxins from his tonsils, so he had recovered rapidly and did not need the surgery.

The response of the community was gratifying, for when the people came to sign up for the lessons, there were fifty-five students, too many for one class; so Mrs. Takata divided them into several smaller ones. When she had completed the teaching, she was told this was only the beginning of Reiki in that area and they asked her to return every six months to conduct further classes.

Many of the people were farmers in this part of the island, and this was cowboy country, as well, with a very large cattle ranch nearby; so the classes she taught had far-reaching effects. The farmers energized their seeds and plants with Reiki, producing bountiful crops. The chicken farmers used it to increase their success by placing their hands in the brooders with the baby chicks each day for fifteen minutes, so the flocks were healthy, with minimal loss. Even the egg production of the hens increased. The cowboys experienced benefits, too, as they worked with the cattle. They reported almost no loss of calves since they began to hold the newborn animals and vitalize them with Reiki; and they also worked with success on the less productive cows, giving them treatment so there would be more calves for the ranch.

In 1939 she traveled again from Honolulu to the Big Island, first teaching in Kona and, on a later visit, in Pahoa. Her first year as a practitioner had been a busy one, so when she received a call from two school teachers on the Big Island of Hawaii asking if she would take a short vacation and visit them, this was a welcome invitation. They had seen the Honolulu newspaper articles and were interested in learning more about Reiki.

When she arrived by boat she was met in Hilo by one of the teachers, and as they drove toward her home, this woman asked many questions about Reiki. At one point along the way she stopped at a residence where she had an errand, and as they entered the yard Mrs. Takata noticed a sign offering the house and lot for sale.

The old man who lived there was alone playing a card game, and when Mrs. Takata was introduced as being from Honolulu, he misunderstood and thought she was interested in the property. He threw his cards into the air, rejoicing that she was going to buy his house. The teacher was very embarrassed and did not know what to say, so Mrs. Takata told him she had not brought a down payment since she had not planned to buy real estate. His response was, "Who is talking about a down payment?" All he required was a monthly sum to provide his income.

It was a beautiful property with an acre of land and a well-built four bedroom house and half basement. There was a large garage in back and adjoining quarters for a maid. As she looked about, she realized that with some repairs and alterations, this house was large enough for a Reiki center, as well as providing private living quarters for the family. She made a quick decision to accept his terms since she could manage the price he was asking. This would enable her to bring her parents and other family members from Kauai to live with her and her daughters in this lovely place, so it seemed appropriate to move to Hilo from Honolulu.

Feeling as though she owned a palace, she found carpenters to begin the alterations, creating not only a home but also a healing center for those who needed help. Before the carpentry was finished, before she could even get settled with furniture in the house, the two school teachers came each day for treatment. When they began to get well, they asked to join her next Reiki class, so her acceptance in Hilo was immediate.

When the building project was completed, she had two treatment rooms, a large waiting room, and the private living area for the family. She hired a yard boy to tend the garden, so within a short time a transformation had taken place with this property and she was ready to offer Reiki to the Big Island.

People from all over the island were soon coming to her for treatments, and she was teaching classes, as well. Almost overnight she had become popular, due mainly to the manager of one of the sugar plantations. He had fallen from his horse, injuring himself and creating problems for his legs and back, so he asked her to come and try to give him relief from the pain. She requested thirty days to work on him, to which he agreed, and on the twenty-ninth day he was fully recovered from his accident.

Since the plantation he managed included several villages, his influence was very great. He was so pleased with his recovery that he offered to send her into these villages to gives lectures and demonstrations, after which she could teach classes; so he called in his staff to help organize these visits. They hired the little sampan bus to transport her to the various club houses where the people had gathered, and in this way Reiki spread throughout the area, with many learning to do it for themselves.

At one of these demonstrations was a blacksmith from the plantation. He was suffering from a piece of steel which the doctor had been unable to remove from his eye, and he asked if she would use him as a model and release this steel as it was very painful. The area was bandaged, so she worked on his eyes and head for about twenty minutes, placing her hands on top of the gauze. When he blinked, there was no pain, and the next morning when he went to the doctor there was no sign of the steel. It was gone. With only that one treatment, the foreign body was removed. This amazed the students in the class and gave them much confidence in Reiki, for although the treatment was given from on top of the bandage, it was effective.

When she went to another village to conduct classes, the minister of the church came to her, telling of a man who had been bedridden for several years, unable to walk after an accident which injured his back. He had read about Reiki in the newspaper articles and wanted very much to meet Mrs. Takata. There was one problem, the minister explained. This man lived a long distance up into the mountains, with the road going only a short distance. The rest of the trip would be by horseback. She was not a good rider, but was willing to give it a try; so they drove for half an hour in the car, then followed the trail for two hours more on the horses.

This family was very happy they had come, and after lunch she began the treatment on the injured man. With so much time on his hands, he read many magazines and newspapers, so he was well versed in Reiki from the articles in the Honolulu paper and asked many questions. She told him she was not the healer. The real healer is Reiki, and Reiki is God Power; so this would determine how well he responded.

They discussed the accident which had left him

paralyzed from the waist down. His upper body was all right, but he had no feeling in the lower half and could not walk. Since the wife served as his nurse and helper, she, too, was confined to their home by his condition; so it was suggested this would be a good time for her to take the Reiki lessons and learn how to give treatment. During the five days Mrs. Takata stayed with them, the wife worked with her and mastered the art of healing with Reiki. The sense of feeling began to return to the husband's body, so they knew he was responding well and there was hope of recovery. Other family members later took the training so they could help whenever they visited, and with daily treatments from his family, in less than a year this man was able to walk about his house and garden with only a cane to steady him.

Naturally, many people heard about these cases and wanted to learn more. Even the staff at the plantation hospital became interested and opened their doors to Reiki, offering a place to conduct classes.

Mrs. Takata's clinic in Hilo thrived, and she was very busy doing treatments there, as well as traveling throughout the islands teaching Reiki classes. There were rewarding reports wherever she went, demonstrating many times the truth that Reiki works on everything that has life—on plants, fowls and animals, as well as human beings.

In early 1940 she had a vivid dream in which she saw Dr. Hayashi in a formal kimono of white silk.

He walked back and forth three times, and she could hear the swish of the silk upon the tatami mats. It seemed to be real, not a dream. This disturbed her, so she wrote inquiring about him, and was reassured when she learned all was well.

A few weeks later she felt an urgency to go to Japan, and when she arrived in April, the Hayashis were very surprised to see her. The Grand Master's greeting puzzled her when he said although he had wanted her to come some time that year, she had arrived too soon. He suggested she go to Kyoto and study hydrotherapy, which would be helpful in her Reiki practice. Mrs. Hayashi spoke privately to her and explained that her husband had decided to go into transition on his own accord. He had not yet set the date, so when Mrs. Takata received a wire from them, she should come immediately to Atami where they would be staying.

Mrs. Takata proceeded to Kyoto for the training in hydrotherapy, and on May 9 when she received the telegram to come at once, she took the night train to Atami, arriving at five A.M. When she reached the Hayashi home she questioned one of the maids as to the health of the Grand Master and learned he was very well, so she was unsure she understood the meaning of "transition" in Japanese.

The family welcomed her at breakfast, and they appeared quite cheerful. Nothing seemed different or unusual until Dr. Hayashi said that starting at ten o'clock that morning there would be many people arriving, and he would like Mrs. Takata to greet them and act as hostess, helping seat the guests. He had invited his friends and students to witness his transition, and he expressed his pleasure that she also would be there for this occasion.

She wondered how anyone could sit and talk so calmly in this way, but Dr. Hayashi said he had already set a time between one and one-twenty P.M., and within that time period he would go into transition. Furthermore, the family had decided that Mrs. Takata would be the proper person to take over his work with Reiki. His daughter was married and did not wish to work; his son wanted to go into business and was not inclined to continue the clinic; and Mrs. Hayashi wanted to retire to her country home. Therefore, they had all agreed that Mrs. Takata was their choice to become the Reiki Grand Master. This was more than an honorary position, for she would be given all the Tokyo property with the clinic and the house; and he had written a document to the Reiki association so the people in Japan would understand that he had chosen Hawayo Takata to be his successor.

Mrs. Takata had been told what was planned, but she found it difficult to believe that a person could go into transition this way, and she thought she had misunderstood. None of the family expressed any sorrow or shed tears, and she was bewildered by it all.

At one o'clock Dr. Hayashi entered the room where

the guests and family were gathered. He was dressed in the same white kimono which Mrs. Takata had seen in her dream, and when he walked across the mats, she could hear the swish of the silk and feel the cool air, just as she had dreamt. He greeted them and explained why he had made this momentous decision.

He knew that war was inevitable between Japan and America, and being a patriotic citizen as well as an Officer in the Naval Reserve, he would be called to active duty aboard a battleship and would have to kill many people. As a devout Buddhist and the Reiki Grand Master, he could not destroy life. He spoke of having lived a life of peace and understanding, of working to help people; so rather than kill others, he had chosen to make a peaceful transition at this time, although he was only sixty-two and in perfect health.

He thanked them for coming, saying this was not death, for life goes on; therefore, transition meant "great change" not death; and there should be no tears or sorrow, for even his family understood and had none. Dr. Hayashi told them the first sign had come, but he felt no pain. Ten minutes later there was another sign, again with no pain. He asked Mrs. Hayashi to position herself behind him, and with the third sign, the Grand Master went into transition peacefully with great dignity, a smile on his face as he fell backward into his wife's waiting arms.

Dr. Hayashi was taken to Tokyo where he lay in state at the Reiki Center and was visited by people from all over Japan who came to express their respect for this great man. For a full week this continued and his body showed no signs of deterioration.

After seven days when the cremation and Zen funeral ceremony were completed, Mrs. Hayashi began packing her belongings to move to her country home. Mrs. Takata had been meditating on her own dilemma, being torn between the two duties of motherhood and Reiki. She asked Mrs. Hayashi's help, proposing that she remain in Tokyo to supervise the clinic and continue the work while Mrs. Takata would return to Hawaii to complete the rearing of her daughters and see them settled in their own homes, after which she would come to Japan to dedicate her life to Reiki.

Mrs. Hayashi was very understanding and agreed to take care of the Reiki center, so Mrs. Takata returned to Hawaii knowing she had left this work in good hands. With the coming of World War II, their communication was broken and it was several years after the war before Mrs. Takata returned to Tokyo for a visit.

She found Mrs. Hayashi in the same place, but great changes had occurred. This was the only building in the area which was untouched by devastation, with it remaining in perfect condition while there was only rubble and debris all around as far as the eye could see. The scars of war on the city were very deep, and during the occupation all possible spaces had been commandeered for refugee housing, so Mrs. Hayashi's private quarters had been given to shelter several families. She had moved into the clinic area, converting it into living spaces for more refugees, particularly orphaned teen-age girls to whom she taught skills such as sewing which permitted them to earn their living honestly.

Mrs. Hayashi was very apologetic that she had been unable to continue the Reiki work and expressed her concern that the Grand Master would disapprove; but Mrs. Takata knew she had done her best simply to survive and only had admiration for her courage. She formally returned the property to Mrs. Hayashi, telling her not to shed any more tears over it, as she would go back to Hawaii and spread Reiki to the world from the center there. Thus, through the intervention of a war, the Usui System of Natural Healing, Reiki, was no longer centered in Japan.

After almost a decade of success with her healing center at Hilo, Mrs. Takata returned to Honolulu where she made her home for the next thirty years, and there she continued her work with Reiki. Maintaining a treatment center in this city, she also traveled among the islands, conducting classes as usual and making an occasional trip to the American Mainland; but the greater emphasis was in Hawaii where she had hundreds of Reiki students.

During the fall of 1973 she was invited to teach a large group on an island off the coast of Washington state, and this was the start of seven very busy years. As the requests for classes began to fill her schedule, she traveled to the Pacific Coast, the Mid-West, East, South, Southwest and into Canada; and with these demands, there was less and less time for the clinic work. The teaching had become a full-time occupation.

As the groups continued to grow in size and number, she was unable to keep up with the requests for lessons. The need for more teachers was obvious, so she began training some of her students and had initiated twenty-two of them as Reiki Masters by the time she went into transition in December, 1980.

CHAPTER FIVE

Even in the eighth decade of her life, Mrs. Takata was a very attractive woman, small boned, less than five feet in height, and weighing slightly over ninety pounds. Her motions were quick and decisive, and she moved with the ease of a young person, upright and graceful. In these later years she still had fresh smooth skin, like that of a child, with few lines and wrinkles in her face. Her gray hair was the only betraying sign of age.

Her appearance belied her years and few people, upon meeting her for the first time, would have suspected she was an octogenarian. One such person was an official in charge of senior citizen discounts on the tickets he was selling, who accepted her word that she was eligible for this consideration, but he flatly refused to believe she was almost eighty years old—sixty-five, perhaps, but not eighty!

She not only taught Reiki; she lived it. Her life was an exceptional demonstration of dedication to the Ideals and Principles of Reiki taught by the Grand Masters who preceded her. She truly cared for people, often putting their welfare and comfort before her own; and she offered treatment freely to those she met along the way, at times for only a few minutes. "Better some Reiki than none at all," she would say.

She was very aware of hands, hers being quite small, and upon one occasion commented on the large size of one student's hands, "Oh, what wonderful Reiki hands! You can cover so much area at one time!" Small hers may have been, but they were powerful. She was a clear channel for the transmission of this healing energy, bringing forty-five years of daily experience to her work.

She lived quite simply, advocating a diet with many fresh vegetables and fruits, whole grains, fish and chicken, and although she would eat red meats, she did so sparingly. Her favorite "home remedy" was a mixture of fresh vegetables—water cress, beets, carrots, and celery—which she pureed in the blender and carried with her on her travels. She often recommended this juice to others, saying it was an excellent blood builder which energized the whole body.

Golfing, at which she was quite accomplished, was her favorite exercise, and when she was in Honolulu she walked to the golf course each morning to play. She liked to travel and especially enjoyed sightseeing in new areas she had not previously visited, often seeking out the local golf courses.

In the way of many who have known poverty and difficult times, Mrs. Takata was quite conservative in money matters. She had worked very hard and earned her own way in life, and as she became more affluent, her habits of economy remained deeply ingrained. She spent very little on her wardrobe, and although she dressed neatly, often colorfully, it was without stylish distinction.

Those who knew her well realized she did not interpret the Spiritual Precept, "Just for today, do not anger," to mean that she should never anger. She had a healthy temper and at times would display it, but these times were few and involved only extreme conditions. When these did occur, she immediately responded, saying what needed to be said, doing what needed to be done to clear the air and restore balance. Her way was to take care of it *today* and not carry such energy over to the morrow.

Mrs. Takata's life was not easy, being filled with many obstacles and responsibilities which she turned into opportunities for growth. She worked very hard, suffered grief and sadness, overcame these difficulties, and in the process, developed great strength. Although her social demeanor was quiet and unassuming, with the politeness of a well-bred Japanese lady, by no means could she be considered weak. She knew what she wanted and she always figured out a way to achieve her goals.

She had a lively personality with the simplicity and open curiosity of a child, asking questions and exploring new ideas, ever probing and learning. She combined this simplicity with an insight which is found only in wisdom, so to those with whom she felt a close connection, she offered advice. A student in one of her early classes remembers her not only as his Reiki teacher but also as a woman who would give him lectures, counseling him for hours when he felt he had been demoted and wanted to quit his job, telling him, "You can't let things get you down. . . . You are more valuable as an outdoor man; a town job is not your way. . . . Always have in your mind to do good things. . .also in the community; then you will get ahead and you will be respected."

Her personal conversation was filled with admonitions, and she advised one student, "If you plan to remarry, marry a young man. If you marry an old one, he'll just get sick and then you will have to take care of him."

She often reminded her classes to give thanks and to express gratitude for all they received. One student took this to heart, saying one must always be aware that Reiki was a gift from God and whenever healing occurred, the practitioner could not take any credit for it. Mrs. Takata smiled, palms together, and quietly responded, "God does not care if you brag —*a little*."

As a teacher, she spoke simply and with power, "This is the way you do Reiki!" Yet, those who participated in more than one class found that she adjusted her instruction for each group, never presenting the information in the same way twice. At times she would tell her students to start the treatment with the head; at other times she would tell them to start with the abdomen; or she might say it really did not matter where they started so long as the complete treatment was given. She encouraged them to develop their intuitive "feel" for Reiki and to do what seemed right for them individually, while observing the basic hand placements which she taught.

Her method of presentation was an oral one, combined with demonstration, and she did not encourage note-taking, saying, "Just do it! Do Reiki, Reiki, Reiki, and then you shall *know*!" She was a strict teacher, and should students be so rude as to whisper in class, she did not hesitate to draw them back to the business at hand, clapping her hands together and saying imperiously, "Students! Pay attention to what I am saying!"

She had a ready smile with a quiet humor, finding much to amuse her in life. Because she was very alert and quick-witted, little escaped her attention. An excellent judge of people, her assessments were at times uncomfortably accurate, although she seldom voiced publicly any personal criticism. Instead, she focused upon the positive and offered compliments whenever possible.

Along with her strength came an implacable quality where Reiki was concerned. She allowed most of the foibles of humanity to flow by without comment, but she did not accept any nonsense in the discussion of Reiki. She took her work very seriously, clarifying without hesitation the misconceptions held by another. When she shook her finger at someone, it emphasized her convictions gained through many years of experience, and there was no arguing with her on this subject—she was the authority and there was no mistaking it.

CHAPTER SIX

No one has been able to explain exactly what Reiki is; however, it is neither electrical nor magnetic in nature. Mrs. Takata emphasized it is simple, it is natural, it is scientific. There is no magic involved, no "hocus pocus," nor is there a need to create an altered state of consciousness in order to do this work. It is well to remain focused on the treatment, but Reiki will work automatically whenever the hands are applied to the area of need.

She called this energy by various names: God Power; Cosmic Energy; Universal Life Force; Radionic Waves; Etheric Waves; Prana; Mana. She likened it to a broadcast from a radio transmitter, unseen, unheard until a receiver picks it up and converts it into sound. In the same way, Reiki is always present and we are unaware of it until the contact is made through the training, after which it can be received and converted into healing energy.

Reiki is not a technique or a method or a process; it just is. In an intellectual sense, Reiki cannot be "taught," for the role of the Master is to empower the student, with the energy being transferred during the four brief ceremonies called "initiations." These initiations open certain inner centers of the body so the energy can be channeled easily and safely. Once the contact has been made and the energy transferred through the touch of the Master, the flow is sensed in the hands, being felt usually as heat, sometimes as a vibration or tingling, occasionally in another form. Each person is unique, and there are infinite expressions of this Universal Life Force.

Instruction is given then in the use of this energy. Specific hand positions are taught for the sake of expedience since long practice has shown these to work efficiently; however, there is no "wrong" way to do Reiki—and, thus, no "right" way.

When the training is completed, the energy is always "on," so the only decision a student makes is whether or not to give the treatment. The practitioner has no control over what will happen, as the responsibility for whatever occurs lies with the one being treated. This is not a conscious mental decision, but one which resides deeply within and involves choices from a level beyond intellectual structuring. It is the body's own wisdom which determines whether or not it will accept the healing energy, the amount and duration of the transmission, and what it will do with this. The practitioner does not create this energy, but is simply the channel through which it is transferred; and in accepting this role of vessel, there is no attachment to results. One does not become a healer, for *Reiki* is the healer.

Mrs. Takata taught that Reiki is harmless and cannot hurt anyone; it does not destroy but, instead, builds and protects. It will vitalize all forms of life—

plants, animals, fish, fowl, and humans from infancy to old age—and it can do only good.

It will work through all fibers, so it is unnecessary for one to disrobe in order to receive a treatment. As the hands are placed over areas of need, the Reiki is unhampered by layers of clothing. It will also pass through wood, metal, casts, even rubber. With the Second Degree training, one does not even have to touch the person being treated, for this energy can be directed to any place at a distance.

Ailments and conditions are labeled either chronic or acute. The chronic ones are of longer standing and likely will require long-term treatment. They have not developed overnight and much Reiki will be needed to bring the body back into balance. Most adults have toxic conditions which need to be cleared from the body before the healing can be completed, so a reaction occurs. This cleansing often brings discomfort, such as headache, nausea, or diarrhea, as the body rids itself of this toxic material; and these are positive signs that indicate the healing is moving forward. The acute cases such as accidents and sudden illness recover much more quickly, often with one treatment, and the reactions are not so severe.

Several conditions are needed to provide an effective channel for this energy. The most important is that one must believe it, for to doubt and not accept Reiki reduces the ability to work with it. The people being treated do not have to hold such belief, as this is not a test of their faith; but the practitioner must believe. Secondly, it must be used. Just as an unused muscle will atrophy, so, too, will Reiki weaken and fade away when it is not exercised. In using it, this must be only for the purpose of helping and healing. There is an inherent wisdom in Reiki which will not permit it to be misused, and it will disappear of its own accord if there is any abuse.

In essence Reiki is unlimited, drawing from the inexhaustible store of Universal Energy, yet there are times when it appears not to bring about a cure. Mrs. Takata taught that diseases which have been diagnosed "terminal," being in their latter stages, usually will not be reversed. These are chronic cases and there is insufficient time to complete the healing; however, the transition is made easier by lowering stress and reducing pain, and this is a great comfort. It will not remove birth defects, nor will it grow a new organ which has been removed surgically, but it will bring relief from the symptoms resulting from these conditions.

The over-all effect of Reiki is to help bring the body into balance so it can heal itself, and this works as well on one's own self as it does with others. Mrs. Takata stressed the need to work first with self. "You are Number One!" she would say, "Then if you have time, treat your family and your friends; but in Reiki, you first, then other people."

"Reiki is natural," she would declare, and nothing unnatural occurs during the healing, although it may be accelerated dramatically. When an organ or gland is operating below par, this energy works to stimulate its natural function. Diabetics, for example, note how quickly their insulin intake is reduced when Reiki is applied. Broken bones knit very rapidly, telescoping the process from months into weeks.

Since Reiki means "Universal Life Energy," it is the essence of life itself and all are born with it. In the Usui System of Natural Healing, contact is made with this universal force, which then works automatically to heal the person on all levels; and those who take this training soon realize it is an invaluable investment, for it is everlasting, instantly available, and helps to raise the level of one's vitality for physical and mental health, as well as enhancing spiritual awareness. Mrs. Takata often spoke of becoming a "complete whole," for we must have not only physical well-being but mental and spiritual balance, as well. Only then can we say we are whole—this is what we receive from Reiki, which she called God Power.

Mrs. Takata emphasized several characteristics which distinguish Reiki, telling her students:

—Everyone has this potential. We are all composed of this Universal Energy and can use it for healing. It is a matter of choice.
—You can treat yourself, as well as others.
—You do not become depleted when treating others. As you give Reiki, you also receive it

and become energized, for you are working with Universal Life Force, not your personal energy.

—You become a channel for healing and take neither credit nor responsibility for results.

—You do not take on the symptoms of those you are treating.

Mrs. Takata taught it is not necessary to know anatomy in order to treat with Reiki, since the hands will respond when they locate the source of the problem and the student does not have to analyze what to do. She encouraged the development of this as an intuitive art, not a rigid system, saying, "Reiki will guide you. Let the Reiki hands find it. They will know what to do."

Although she knew anatomy, she sometimes used fanciful names for certain areas, such as the solar plexus which she called the "Big Motor," saying it was the main center from which energy flows to other parts of the body. She emphasized treating the abdomen, the Foundation Treatment, teaching that most ailments and disharmonies in the body originate here from poorly functioning organs with low vitality.

She often spoke of the need to find the cause of the condition, for it was not enough to treat only the effect: "Find the cause and you will remove the effect." Most people come for help because they have a symptom, and it is well to put the hands upon that specific area to relieve the pain and discomfort; however, it is better to do the complete treatment and let Reiki discover what is causing the problem, which may or may not be located in the same place. Only when the cause is removed will the benefit of treatment be long lasting. If poor health habits such as faulty nutrition and lack of exercise are involved, it will be necessary to change these patterns if there is to be progress, for Reiki will give only temporary relief in these cases.

In her classes she demonstrated the proper hand positions for the complete treatment, and she noted there are three major areas to be considered: the front, especially the abdomen; the head; and the back. Here are found all the organs and glands, as well as the major systems, so a treatment will vitalize the entire body. The order in which the Reiki is done does not matter, so long as the full treatment is given, but it usually starts with the head or the abdomen. If there is a specific need to work on the arms, legs, or other parts of the body, the hands are placed directly on that area.

She would tell her students, "Except for shock or accident, use the full treatment, and this is the same for all things. Don't try to take only the parts. The body is a complete unit, so whenever possible, treat it completely. Start with the abdomen or the head—it doesn't matter—then proceed with the whole treatment. It is the same for all, whether physical or mental. There is no difference in the treatment." At times this is not possible and she would advise, "Do what you can. Some Reiki is better than none at all."

Phyllis Lei Furumoto and Hawayo Takata
1980

Phyllis Lei Furumoto

CHAPTER SEVEN

All great teachers use a similar pattern—they tell stories—and Mrs. Takata was such a teacher, leaving a rich legacy of her forty-five years of Reiki experience. She shared these with each class, and as the beginning students listened, many thought them preposterous . . . yet . . . something about this little woman was so genuine, so sincere, that these stories could not be dismissed lightly as mere fantasy, nor even as puffed-up versions of the actual happening. They had the ring of truth, even as she exuded that same quality of believability.

The basic life values held by Mrs. Takata were quite traditional, and she was a person with substance—solid, balanced, and grounded; so as these students began to work with Reiki, many discovered through their own experiences that she had not only told the truth, she had not told the half of it. Her stories were entertaining, but they were neither false nor fanciful. She had told it like it was.

In order to feel the essence of this great teacher, let the stories be told in her words, using her expressions and language patterns.

Asthma/Emphysema

I was called to a private home late one night because the guest was having difficulty breathing with asthma. I gave her two hours of treatment, from ten P.M. to midnight, and she began to feel better, with the tension and cough going away. When I left she was breathing easy and said, "I feel like my old self." Altogether I gave this lady four treatments, but I had success with many cases of asthma and also with emphysema.

Leprosy

After this lady went home I began to work on the host of this household. He seemed like a strong man, large and healthy, and he was well-liked, being always pleasant and kind. I noticed he always wore a jacket and a neckerchief, fully covered up no matter what the weather, hot or cold, sunny or wet. Even his hands were covered, for he always wore gloves.

When some friends saw me going to and from that house, they warned me it was not safe to go there; so I said, "Is that so?"; and as I got to know this family, I learned there was a disease which affected the man's mother and his brothers and sisters. Even at this time his young brother was on Molokai at the leper colony. This was a new experience for me and I wanted to help these people. I asked him to change his diet—to eat no red meat or pork, only light white fish, seaweed, herb tea, and a quart of vegetable juice daily—a mixture of cress, carrot, celery and beet to purify his blood. Along with this I did Reiki every day, and what a change in three months! These treatments had brought back his health. He now wore short sleeved shirts with the neck open, no neckerchiefs or jackets. He took off the gloves and his fingernails were in excellent shape. His eyebrows had grown back and the puffiness was gone from his body. He was in perfect physical condition, with no more leprosy.

Accidents

There was a young boy who appeared always to be in trouble. It was never his fault but he seemed to pull problems to him. His parents were concerned and told me, "Everything he does seems to bring bad luck." He was a kind boy and a good student, and he did not want to be negative; he just could not seem to help himself. He offered to assist the newsboy in delivering the papers and was shown how to throw the newspaper onto the porch. When he did this, the paper bounced on the step and went through the front window. When he tried to play ball at school and swung the bat, it hit another boy in the face. Such things happened to him all the time. None of this was intentional, all accidental, but they felt sorry for him and wanted to know if Reiki could help him. I assured them this could occur because Reiki would give him higher vibrations, and the quality of this energy would cause these accidents to stop, so we should try it. When I was confronted with new experiences, something I had not met before, I always said it is best to try and then we will find out if Reiki will work. This boy responded very well to Reiki, so he was vitalized and the accidents stopped. All the negative experiences left him and he became an honor student.

Tumors

There was a woman who had to stop teaching school because of her physical condition. For three years she had been unable to work because of a large tumor. She began treatment with Reiki, and for the next three weeks she felt no pain and had no temperature, but she felt something stirring inside and began to pass chunks of tissue. I said, "The Reiki is working! This is what it does, removing every foreign body." She felt very healthy and normal, and when after twenty-one days the activity in her abdomen had stopped and everything had cleared, she weighed herself and discovered she had lost thirty-five pounds. When her doctor checked her, he found the tumor was gone, and she was happy the surgery was unnecessary. I had great success with tumors, but no others were as large as that one. There are many types of tumors, and sometimes if it is solid, it is well to have the surgery to remove it.

Baldness

When the war broke out on December 7, 1941, I received a call from a family who lived near Pearl Harbor. They wanted me to come help their son who was twenty-one years old. He had been asked by the army to help in the clean-up after the enemy planes had attacked. Many soldiers were caught unawares and the army needed volunteers to pick up the broken bodies. This young man was one of the helpers and he was very shocked emotionally by what he saw. When he went home at the end of the day, he went upstairs to wash his hands for dinner, and when he did not come down for a long time, his father checked to see what was keeping him. He found his son standing in front of the mirror with his comb and brush. When he had combed his hair, the comb was filled with hair; when he had brushed it, the brush was also filled. The more he combed, the more it came out. Finally, he was completely bald and in such shock he did not know what to do. His parents tried to console him, and his mother made a little cap for him to wear. They felt very sorry for him and decided to call me for help.

I came as soon as I could from Hilo and went to their home, prepared to stay awhile, for hair could not be made to grow overnight. First, the shock would have to be be released; then the body would need to receive Reiki treatments every day, so I suggested this would be a good time for all the family to have the lessons so these could continue when I was gone. The family was very happy to do this and from the next day, the parents were helping me with the treatments.

After about two months the young man's hair began to grow back, and in six months he had a complete head of hair, very normal, except in his black hair there were small patches of white, for the shock was very great.

* * *

In another case involving hair, a lady came back to Honolulu from the Mainland and called me for treatments. She said she had tried all kinds of hair remedies, tonics, and massages but nothing helped, so she had to wear a little bonnet to cover her bald head. She had taken lessons from me six years before, and she felt that now only Reiki could help her. Before I accepted her, I wanted to know something about her. I knew she had separated from her husband before leaving Hawaii, and I also knew that Reiki would not work unless we removed the cause, so I asked, "Did you come back to get help for your hair problem, or did you just come back to get more money from him? If this is the case, no Reiki!" After thinking it over for a few days, she called to say she was accepting Reiki completely and she did not have negative feelings toward her husband. I took her for treatment since she had purified herself and cleared her mental side; and in only one week her body had a cleansing reaction. In only two months her hair was beginning to grow, and within six months it was normal.

* * *

There was another young man—a wonderful pianist—and he had beautiful straight black hair which was falling out every time he combed it. He came for treatment and I discovered his kidneys were the cause. He had the complete treatments and after one month, when his kidneys began to function better, the hair stopped falling out. He became a student of Reiki and took responsibility for healing himself, so his story had a happy ending, too.

* * *

There was another outstanding case with a man who was very bald, just like a billiard ball, he said. He joked about it, but he felt it was too far gone to be helped. His wife encouraged him, and they both took the Reiki class, so I gave him a few treatments and left the rest to them. Since he had had no shock or accident, I recommended he concentrate more on the vital organs, as well as the head. After about four months, he was very happy to see blond fuzz, like a baby chick, all over his bald spot, and soon he had a full head of hair which made him very happy.

Children

There were many couples who were childless and wanted to have a family, so it was a good thing for them both to come for treatment. It was even better for them to take the lessons so they could keep up the energy and be vitalized. Many times this was all they needed to have a child, and one lady, when her husband wanted to give her a present at the birth of their first baby, asked for Reiki treatments instead so she could be strengthened immediately after childbirth. They even asked me to be the second godmother for their little girl, and I was most honored to do this.

These babies who had had Reiki before they were born were very healthy, and their mothers had easy labors. Some of them even told me they had no pain during labor, and it seemed very easy when they were receiving Reiki during this period. In the classes I lectured on how easy the birth would be if they had received their treatments during pregnancy so their organs would be functioning well. I said many times if they used Reiki and the body was in good condition, they would have painless childbirth.

There were times when the mother had difficulty carrying the child, and she would miscarry. The best plan is to start Reiki before becoming pregnant, and then have treatments to strengthen her during the pregnancy; and if any symptoms then appear, Reiki could be applied immediately.

There was one lady who had miscarried five times, and with her sixth pregnancy, she came to me; so I treated her and changed her diet. I told her to avoid acid food and then Reiki would bring her system back into balance. I worked with her and when the time came, she had a healthy baby boy. She felt fine the entire time, with no morning sickness or grogginess as she had experienced before.

I taught Reiki to one nurse who was a specialist in childbirth and worked for a gynecologist. She was able to tell with the Reiki fingers when the birth would occur, for her hands would receive a little signal when the child was about to come. She enjoyed her work very much and said it was as blessing there was such a thing as Reiki.

Epilepsy

There was a family whose daughter had epilepsy from the age of nine, many seizures a day. The school bus driver did not want to be responsible for her and would not let her ride the bus unless a member of the family accompanied her; otherwise, the family would have to take her in their own car to school. Since the mother had to work in the store and also care for her large family, she could not take this child to school every day; so the daughter stayed home. She was very happy and her playmates were four or five years old.

This went on for ten years and the girl was nineteen when the mother decided if there was anything that could help her daughter, it should be done, so they went to Honolulu to see if the doctors there could add some help. They could offer none, saying it was too late. She even brought in a Kahuna, the Hawaiian medicine man, and his helpers for a ceremony, but this did nothing for her, either.

Finally someone told her of Mrs. Takata and she came to me immediately, so I said, "If you will have the patience to try Reiki for one year, I will accept her; and after a few treatments, if you think this is going to help, I would like you and some other members of the family to take lessons so you can give her more than one treatment a day." She agreed to that, even if it took a year, saying, "From nine to nineteen is a long, long time for a person to suffer, so what is one year of my life?"

The girl was brought every morning for a week and then she began to have the reaction. Usually she had two or three fainting spells at night, but with the reaction, she had seven or eight, so the family got little sleep. I said, "That is too bad she suffers even more, but this is necessary in order to clear the toxins from her system. This is the way Reiki works, and she will begin to feel better after this cleansing."

The mother was willing to do anything that might assist, so she changed her daughter's diet, removing the ice cream and cake and cookies; and after the reaction was completed, the girl began to feel better and her seizures were fewer and fewer. We began the treatments in October and by the Spring I said she did not have to come to me any more, for the family could treat her at home. She continued to improve, and in this way she was entirely cured of epilepsy. Without seizures, she was able to live a normal life and could help around the house, cooking and sewing, things she had never been able to do before; and the whole family was grateful.

* * *

In one case of epilepsy, the lady had such severe attacks that she was unable to go out alone. It was feared she might fall with a seizure and injure herself, so she wanted to try Reiki.

She came daily for treatment for thirty days, and during this time she and her husband took the classes so they could continue the treatment at home. She began to recover very rapidly after the reaction had removed the toxins from her body, and as she progressed, the seizures became lighter and lighter, so in three months she no longer suffered from this condition.

She had come to me only a month, and the rest was done between her and her husband. She was healed completely and never had another seizure.

Accidents

This was a large family, and one of the sons had an accident one morning when he was on his way to the cane field carrying a five-gallon sprayer full of weed killer. He slipped and fell, and the force of his fall caused the sprayer to open and spray the herbicide into his eyes. He tried to push it away but it was too late, so he rushed to the plantation dispensary. The doctor was very concerned, saying that even one drop of this poison could hurt the eyes, so he treated and bandaged them, sending some pain killers home with the injured man and hoped for the best.

As soon as the family got him home, they called me, "This is an emergency, Mrs. Takata. Can you come right away?" I was very busy with a roomful of people waiting for treatment that morning, so I told them I would come as soon as possible, but in the meantime for the family to begin treating him, lightly putting their hands on top of the bandaged eyes and giving him Reiki. "You can do the same treatment as I can because Reiki is the same, whether it is you or me."

The mother and daughter and their neighbors who had all taken the lessons took turns giving treatment, so he was receiving Reiki every minute, starting immediately after the accident. When I arrived at the afternoon, he was still sound asleep, having slept all day, and when he awoke at four o'clock, he was very hungry. He remembered the accident but felt no pain or discomfort; he just wanted to eat.

The next morning he went back to the doctor who found it difficult to accept the young man's word that he had taken no pain killers and had suffered no pain. He didn't quite know how to explain to the doctor about the Reiki treatments. When the bandage was removed, the eyes were still red but there was no loss of vision. That was the last day he had to wear a bandage and every day he received many hours of Reiki, so he recovered fully.

Any time there is an accident, it will be necessary to treat the affected part, but also release the shock from the adrenals in the back, and give the complete treatment to vitalize the whole body with Reiki. There will be a very fast recovery from an accident if Reiki is started immediately.

* * *

One day I had a call from a lady who had just had an automobile accident and received a whiplash.

Someone had bumped her from behind and she wanted to come for immediate treatment. I worked on her for two hours on the affected part—the head, the back of her neck and shoulders—then I did the complete treatment to release the tension and shock. This took a long time but she went home happy, knowing she could come back the next day if she had any pain; but she phoned, saying she was fine and did not need another treatment. Whenever you work immediately after an accident, there is very fast relief and repair.

* * *

Another lady came for help after an accident, but this had happened one and a half years before. She had a whiplash and had worn a thick collar for two months. She thought she was well but whenever she drove the car, she experienced great fear and was scared to drive. Because she had this for a long time, it was a chronic case and would take more treatments. She was willing to come as many times as necessary, and we were able to release the shock and tension, so she made a full recovery.

Arthritis/Rheumatism

Some people came with arthritis; others said they had rheumatism. The words may differ but the treatment is the same. The complete treatment is given, but in these cases we start with the abdomen. When all these organs are balanced and vitalized, much of the cause is eliminated. Then we work directly on the area of the pain. A change of diet is also needed, for what you eat is very important.

No matter how severe the pain, the person will begin to feel better after a few treatments—I would say eight days—four days of treatment and then four to recuperate, followed by the additional treatments as needed.

Sometimes accidents can cause the beginning of this pain. When you are young and have a little bump, you ignore it and have no patience to allow it to heal completely; but perhaps twenty-five years later when toxins begin to settle in this weak spot, then it begins to ache. When the pain starts and you feel uncomfortable, it is chronic already.

With Reiki there is always hope. As long as there is life and willingness to spend the time for treatments, there shall be help. The recovery may be inch by inch, like peeling off a layer of paint, but no matter how deeply the cause is buried, Reiki will reach it and remove it.

* * *

When I had my studio in Hilo, a lady came from eighty miles away and said she had very painful rheumatism, suffering aches and pains all night and day. She could hardly walk for the pain. When I gave her Reiki, I found that every organ was depleted; and the treatment took two hours the first time. She was mostly concerned with her feet because it hurt so much when she walked, so I worked on them and told her the puffiness and swelling would go away, but she would have to change her diet a little and remove the sweets—no cake or candy. She needed a cleanser to help get this water out of her body, so she should take limes from her tree and squeeze them into warm water—about six glasses a day.

She came on the bus every day for two weeks and by that time she had lost quite a bit of weight and felt much better from all the Reiki. Since eighty miles was a long way to come each day, I encouraged her to learn this art for herself so she could do a daily treatment on herself and come to me only once a week. After two months she did take the training and when the holidays came, she brought me some special bread, saying this was the first time in many years she had been able to knead the dough and she wanted to share the bread.

* * *

There was a man who had arthritis so badly he was in the hospital for five months, but they could do nothing for him and finally sent him home. He was a large man—two hundred seventy-five pounds—and when he came to me for treatment, he brought a driver to help him walk to my house. When they reached my steps, this man could not lift his feet six inches, so I stopped him, saying, "This is impossible. It is too hard for you to even lift your feet, so how can I put you on the treatment table? You have to go home. . ." and when I said "home," this big man began to cry, so I continued, "I have not finished my sentence. I am going to go along to give you treatment in your own home. That way we don't have to get you up and down the steps." "You are very kind. I thought you had given up hope for me."

So I went to his home and gave him Reiki, the complete treatment. He said he had had this pain for seven years and he was very grateful that he had hope for results. His wife had tears in her eyes, too, for she wanted to help and was very cooperative. I promised to come every day for a full month, assuring her that if all went well, he would be able to walk without pain.

She was a good helper because she was very religious. She never missed a Sunday going to church, so I asked if her husband went, also. "Not all the time; only if I coax him for a special occasion."

I worked with him and after a week's treatments, he began to change. The reaction set in and everything within him was stirred up, even his circulation. I told him to drink lemon juice in water and to change his diet a little. He could have fish, but less meat; and he needed more fresh vegetables, especially cress and celery which had been pureed. He promised to try anything I suggested and that made the work easier.

In the second week he improved so much he was able to get up and walk around the house. The treatments continued and on the third week, a red spot appeared on his right elbow. This spot grew and grew, and in four days it was like a balloon with liquid inside. He was concerned and asked what was going to happen, and I told him I was just going to treat it and leave it up to Reiki.

After a few days as I was treating this area, it ruptured and began to spurt. I had been expecting this to happen, so I grabbed an old sheet which I had nearby and covered the hole while the liquid drained and drained, along with white clumps that looked like cottage cheese. I told him this was the calcium that was causing all the pain in his joints. It was drawn to this one place to be released from his body, and what a big relief it was to have all these toxins leaving. It took a few days for the hole to completely heal, but the man experienced no pain.

It was very easy for him to walk, so I asked him to go to the doctor while the hole was still open and show him what had happened. The doctor was pleased to see this and to hear of the man's improvement.

By the end of the month this man had lost weight and could walk with absolutely no pain, so I said to him, "Please dress yourself and walk—not ride—with your wife to the church, and you go right down to the front and kneel before the altar and offer your gratitude and thanks to God that you can once more walk without pain." He agreed to do this, and when he began to dress for church he found his suit was too baggy, so he got out the one that he wore for his wedding many years before and it fitted perfectly.

I did not have to go back to his home to give any more treatments for he said he would come to my office once a week. I thought he would come for the rest of the year, but he did not do this for he was too busy playing ball, climbing coconut trees, and fishing with his sons. He did not need any more Reiki.

Reaction

When treated, most chronic illnesses have reaction. The body goes through a cleansing and in some cases the reaction is so great the people complain that instead of getting well, their pain was worse. This means their bodies have accepted Reiki and it is working very well, so we go on treating and giving thanks for this internal cleansing. I tell them to accept the pain because a great change is stirring up and they should continue in order to get this out of their systems. This is very important in Reiki, so whenever there is a reaction they should say, "Thank God it is working!" Have patience and bear it for a few days if necessary, for this is the way Reiki works to cleanse the whole body.

Headaches

There are many causes for headaches. There was a man who suffered from headaches after every dinner, and he did not want to get in the habit of taking pills, so he would drive around before going to bed, trying to get relief from the fresh air. One evening as he drove past my house, he decided to stop because he had heard others talk about Mrs. Takata. He told me he had this headache every night and he didn't know why. I started to treat his abdomen and he objected, saying he had a headache, not a stomach ache; so I explained I was looking for the cause before I went to the affected part. When I got to the gall bladder area there was much vibration in my hands, so I told him perhaps we have found the cause and I continued to work on that area. Then I worked on his head and then the back, doing the complete treatment. When I finished he said this was all very strange because I had concentrated on his stomach and when I came to his head, all the pain was gone. He was very relieved when he left. I talked with his wife and explained it was likely the rich desserts that caused the headaches, so from that time they had no desserts and he had no more headaches.

Burns

I treated many burns, but the worst one was a man, a very strong man, who was an electrician. Early one morning he received a call from the baker saying his oven did not work and he needed to bake his loaves of bread, so please come quickly to fix it. Without checking the switch to see that it was turned off, this electrician crawled into the oven to see what was wrong and when he was inside where the wires were, suddenly there was a flash and he caught fire. The baker pulled him out and smothered the fire on his clothes, but the man was so badly burned they rushed him to the doctor. He was in a very serious condition and unconscious when the sister-in-law and her friends arrived at the hospital—four of them with Reiki training—and they went to work on him immediately. They treated him all over except for one small spot where he was the least burned. In that way he would know how much the Reiki helped. He received treatment until five o'clock that afternoon, when he awakened. He had no pain, although the doctor had said he suffered third degree burns. He was able to go home where the friends helped give him Reiki, Reiki every day until the bandages were removed. He had no scars except for the one spot which they had left untreated, and he could see for himself the difference Reiki made. Then he wanted to take lessons so he would be able to help others as he had been helped.

* * *

There was another case with a burn. A man in one of the villages took the lessons and he offered Reiki for all his neighbors. He wanted to help everyone with this, but one neighbor would not accept it and criticized the one who was trying to do good things with Reiki; but this man just remembered the Ideals and refused to let this criticism worry or anger him.

In this village the children were setting off firecrackers to celebrate the New Year and the young son of the man who was against Reiki was accidentally burned when a firecracker fell into his pocket. He was taken to the hospital and, instead of getting better, he got worse and worse. The burn would not heal.

When the Reiki student went to the hospital to see his friends, he also visited the boy. He put his hands on top of the blanket and as he gave Reiki, he gave a silent prayer that the boy would get better. The pain was less when he finished, so the boy asked him to come again, so the man came many times and soon the healing was completed. Only after the boy returned home did his father learn about the treatments. He felt very humble and grateful that his son was well, so he went to his neighbor and apologized for speaking against Reiki.

* * *

In another case a workman was finishing a roof, using hot tar on the paper. Instead of using a ladle to mix the tar, he put his hand into the mixture and suffered a terrible burn. Then he stuck his hand into a nearby can of kerosene to wash off the tar and began screaming with the pain. He was working at my neighbor's home and I heard him yelling, so I ran to see what was happening. I held his hand and began to treat it with Reiki. We sat on my doorstep for about half an hour until the pain stopped, and then the other workers took him to the doctor to have it bandaged, after which they brought him back. Through the bandage I worked on him another hour, and when he went home he said there was no pain. I treated him every day until the bandage was removed, and his hand was healed completely without a scar.

Tuberculosis

Many people used to have tuberculosis, and I had much experience with these cases. This was very contagious and they did not want to be around their family or friends, so they went to a sanitarium. One man who had been in the sanitarium for several years read about Reiki and sent his wife to see me. She was willing to take the lessons so she could work on him every day during visiting hours, so I agreed to go with her to visit the man and to treat him. We would see then if Reiki might help him recover. He felt he benefited from it, so he asked me to teach his wife. She joined the next class and when she went to the hospital to give him daily treatment, he began to get better.

As he was getting well, he wanted to learn Reiki, too. I told him I could not have a class there in the sanitarium, but he said he wanted the power—that was all he needed from me. His wife was coming every day to work on him and she could show him what to do and would give him the proper information. He already knew where to place his hands from watching her do the treatments, so he only wanted me to come on four days and give him the contact with the Universal Energy. I did this, and they were very happy to be able to work with Reiki.

At the same time I had another case of tuberculosis. This man's wife was my housekeeper and she wanted to take the lessons so she could treat her husband. After only three months of daily treatments, he was discharged from the sanitarium.

There was a young woman who had advanced tuberculosis. Her parents came to me, asking me to treat her. She was engaged to be married and they did not know whether she should marry or if she should cancel the engagement. I went to her home every day for a week and we knew she would benefit from Reiki, so she and her mother and their neighbors took the lessons in order to have many people helping her. In six months she was completely well and could go ahead with the marriage.

Strokes

For strokes, the best thing is to prevent them. In most cases this is caused by high blood pressure, so Reiki helps lower the pressure and the stroke will not occur. However, if the stroke has happened, treatment does not start for twenty-one days in order to give the blood a chance to settle. After three weeks treatment is begun. Do not go to the affected part first; go to the cause. The basic treatment is given—front, back and then the head. Always treat the head, especially down the sides of the neck, to help lower the blood pressure. If daily treatment is given, the person can be helped and will be able to walk again.

In one of my cases, a man was bedridden for sixteen years after a stroke. His daughter was very concerned and when she heard about Reiki, she wanted to give it a try. I worked on him for about three weeks and could tell there was hope, so the daughter took the lessons and treated her father every day. She did well and in a year's time, he was able to walk around his house with only the aid of a cane.

* * *

There was another man who was in a wheelchair for three years after a stroke. He was very depressed, so I worked with him and with his wife, also, for she was tired from having to wait on him. Her attitude was very negative and it affected him, as well. Attitude is very important. If the person has given up and feels there is no hope, this creates difficulty in getting well. After she changed to a more positive attitude, one of thankfulness and gratitude, he made up his mind he was going to get well faster, and in seven days he got up from the wheelchair and could walk.

Multiple Sclerosis

There was a case with M. S., multiple sclerosis, who had been in a wheelchair for several years, and he wanted to know if he would be able to walk again, so I said, "God willing and if you have His blessings, Reiki can do it!"

His housekeeper brought him and she was interested in healing, so she joined a class and mastered this art. I gave him only two weeks of treatment, and after that she took over with Reiki. She also changed his diet, giving him many more fresh vegetables, took away his tobacco and liquor, and concentrated on a healthier lifestyle. For exercise he lowered himself into his pool and moved his arms and legs.

Within a short time he could walk around his house with a cane, and then he called to say he had a class of friends and neighbors. Twenty people took the lessons. He demonstrated how strong he was getting by putting me in his wheelchair and pushing me around the pool. He was making great progress and I told him at that rate, he would be able to go dancing within six months. He even planted a little garden so he could grow his own vegetables and get his exercise at the same time. He was very enthusiastic, with a positive attitude, and did everything I suggested to help him recover.

One day I received a call from his housekeeper. She was very distressed and said she was leaving. Some of the man's friends from the past had moved in, and he had joined them with his old habits—smoking, drinking, eating the wrong kind of food. With no more treatments, within two weeks he had lost all the gain. He could not walk and had to go back to his bed and wheelchair.

Children's Diseases

With children's diseases, Reiki helps the discomfort and also prevents the dangerous side effects. Give the whole treatment, and especially with chicken pox, work on the affected parts so there will be no scars. It is wonderful when the parents learn Reiki, for they have all this help right at hand and can take care of this illness immediately.

I had one severe case of chicken pox which was not a child but a young man who was out of college. His mother called to see if I could help prevent the scars. This was a very gentle young man who wanted to become a professional musician. He was interested in preserving the Hawaiian music, so he had a small group who entertained in the night clubs playing this kind of music. We became friends while I was treating him, and I talked about Reiki, telling him how it would be a very good investment since he traveled with his work, for he would be able to treat his voice and keep it in good condition and he could revive himself when he was tired. When he was well again he appreciated very much there were no pock marks on his face. He took the lessons and became a very good practitioner, for he used it on himself and on his group. His talent grew as he wanted it, so he became a great success creating beautiful music, with many people coming to hear it.

Heart

Heart attacks—naturally, we should keep the blood pressure in order and prevent heart attacks with Reiki. I had a call about my neighbor, telling me to run to her quickly because it looked like she was about to have a heart attack. I said to tell her to lie down on the floor on her back and try to be very calm while I could get there. When I arrived, I knelt beside her and began to treat the solar plexus, not the heart. This is to relieve the pressure first. Then I worked on the rest of the abdomen for about half an hour before I went to the chest. Around the heart area she was very tense, and it was true—she was about to have a heart attack. Then I worked on her head, and the blood vessels on the side of her neck felt stiff, like uncooked macaroni, so I worked there and relaxed them. When they began to soften, the rhythm of her heart beat became normal, and she could breathe properly again.

I told her to have someone take her to the doctor to have her heart checked, and when she returned home I would give her more Reiki. That afternoon I gave her a complete treatment—front, head, back—and she recovered very quickly from this episode.

Tetanus

I was allowed by the doctors to go to the hospital to treat patients who wanted Reiki, and my first case was tetanus—lockjaw. I was called by the attending nurse, and this patient was her father. There did not seem to be any more the doctors could do for him. He was in a coma with his jaws shut tight, and when I felt the solar plexus, it was very stiff, like a board, so it was hard to give him the basic treatment. I worked and worked for about two hours, and finally the abdomen began to feel warm. There were little vibrations in my hands, so I could see the Reiki was taking effect. He came out of his coma, so then I worked on his head and held his tight jaws; and in about fifteen minutes the jaw dropped. He opened his mouth and asked for water.

I gave him two treatments that day, and when I came the next day he was smiling and able to have soup and light nourishment. He improved very rapidly. It was amazing and that was one of my first experiences with severe tetanus.

Addictions

I worked with many people who had bad habits, like alcoholism or smoking. There was no meanness in them, just a bad habit they got into; and these could be adjusted with Reiki because it goes deeper than just the surface. With Second Degree or Intermediate Level of Reiki, it can reach the subconscious and work with that level while the Universal Life Force is applied.

My teacher said that all these things—liquor, alcohol, tobacco, even drugs like cocaine and morphine—were put into the world for a good purpose. When the doctor prescribes them, it works like medicine and will help you. When we use these on our own we are likely to overdose, and then it is like a poison.

When a person comes to the stage of habitual overdosing, it is time to stop or it will ruin the health. By treating physically and mentally with the subconscious mind, Reiki can help. When the person makes up his mind that he wants to quit and asks for Reiki, it will work wonders in a few days with that cooperation. When they desire from their own will to quit, it is much easier with the help of Reiki.

Weight

Many people weigh too much from over eating, while others have disorders of the thyroid and other glands; so all these glands need to be treated. Nothing is impossible, so if you want to lose weight, treat daily with Reiki and adjust the glands. Take the lessons and do it yourself, and when this is done, then push away the table. Strong will power will be needed to have only one serving of food and no rich desserts, but this is necessary. When that is done, exercise is next. Take a walk. Walking is the best exercise, but do it every day, consistently.

Underweight is also a problem for some people, and these same glands need to be adjusted. Reiki helps them work in the opposite direction, and weight can be added when they are in balance and functioning properly.

I have worked with many cases of obesity, and it is usually the thyroid gland which is giving problems, especially with the women. This has been my experience, and sometimes this gland has enlarged so there is a goiter. I have seen goiter as big an an orange sticking out, and when all the glands were adjusted with Reiki, it had shrunken and left no scar. One young lady came to me with an enlarged gland the size of a walnut, and in only twenty treatments she was completely well.

Many people told me this obesity was inherited, their whole family was fat, but I say this is not so—you can adjust yourself by staying on a good diet, with exercise and, most important, with Reiki treatments.

* * *

I had one case where the woman weighed more than three hundred pounds, a beautiful woman who was an entertainer. She was weak from trying to diet, and I suggested she eat raw vegetables to gain vitality and to get her exercise by swimming. With the first Reiki treatment I found her thyroid in poor condition, and she was retaining a lot of liquid because her kidneys were not working properly. She never missed her daily treatment and by the time I left her, she had lost one hundred fifty pounds, her energy was up, and the glands were functioning completely. She had taken the lessons so she could continue to treat herself, and her only complaint was that her costumes no longer fit and had to be made smaller.

Water Retention

Many people have too much water in their systems and when Reiki works on the kidneys, they begin to function better and the liquid starts to leave the body. The ankles and legs will be smaller and the waistline will return.

Respiratory Problems

With all the respiratory problems—emphysema, hay fever, asthma, pneumonia, flu, colds—in all these the mucous comes from the bronchi, so treat the affected area and, if the nasal passage is cleared down to the throat and there is no inflammation, there will be no hay fever or asthma.

* * *

I had one man who came to get help with drainage from his ear. He had been a wrestler and his upper chest had been hurt in one of the matches. This was the beginning of this ear drainage, as well as a little asthmatic wheezing. I had never worked on a chronic ear problem and offered to take the case for one month.

I found that the cause of the problem was in the area of the bronchi and it took the most Reiki, but we also corrected the effect. He came every day and by the end of the month, the problem had cleared up completely. He took the training so he could prevent any further occurrence, and that was the last time I saw him.

In such cases, it is chronic and the treatment is the same—the complete treatment with concentration on the affected area.

* * *

I worked with a man from Maui who had to retire

because of his emphysema. It created such strain on his heart the doctor sent him to a heart specialist in Honolulu, who sent him to the hospital.

His wife took an apartment and went every day to the hospital to visit him. She was not far from my office and heard about Reiki, so she decided to call on me and find out more about it.

After a month her husband was not making any progress, so he was dismissed from the hospital to go home. Instead, his wife took him straight to my office and I met him for the first time. We began his treatment and I found the bronchial area needed much Reiki. On the fourth day of treatment he began to get a reaction, coughing up hard sticky mucous from his lungs. His wife joined the next class of students so she could join me in giving him Reiki, and he showed rapid progress. One day he said there was no more mucous coming up and his breathing was much better without so much strain on his heart. He was on the way to full recovery, so that was a very happy ending with this emphysema.

* * *

I had a case of pneumonia where they took the person to the hospital and gave him oxygen to help his breathing, and then they called for Reiki. I worked on the chest and the pleura and the lungs, treating until the crisis was past. The temperature came down and his whole body was dripping with perspiration. When you work with such an ill person, be very careful not to jar him. You cannot turn him over to work on the back, so just slip the hands underneath and hold them under the body, moving them down from the shoulder to the hip, first on one side and then on the other. This might take about two hours, but usually the fever breaks and the crisis is over. I went about twice in these cases and the person bounced back to health.

Reiki works wonderfully in cases of fever, so do not neglect even a cold when you can help with this energy. It takes only one or two treatments but if you neglect this, the cold can develop into other more serious conditions. I have worked with many pneumonia cases and never lost a one.

Kidney and Gallstones

When kidney stones form from the toxins on the kidney walls, they turn into crystals which are very, very hard. With Reiki, they are sometimes passed and at other times are dissolved so they can be flushed from the body. Reiki can do this, but it takes daily treatment and often patience for this to happen. It took a long time to create these stones, so it might take some time for Reiki to reverse the condition, but this is better than having an operation.

With gallstones, the same thing will happen. The stones will dissolve, but this may take some time.

Bones

When there is a broken bone, it will heal very quickly with Reiki. Do not start the treatment until the bone is set and in the cast. Instead, go to the solar plexus and start working immediately on the tension and to the adrenals to release the shock from the accident. When the cast is ready, go to the affected part and start the Reiki on the break, working from on top of the cast; and it will go through with very good results. Reiki will work through casts or wood or even rubber, anything that is used to help the injury. It will penetrate this material, and the healing will be very rapid.

* * *

I had a good friend who fell on a slippery floor and broke her wrist in three places, and it was very painful. We started treatment the next day, but after two treatments she said since this was going to take several weeks to heal and she did not want to sit around thinking about her broken wrist, how would I like to go with her on a shopping trip. I was very surprised and asked where we would go. Her plan was to go to the Philippines, then to Hong Kong and Thailand, Ceylon (Sri Lanka), and finally, India. She didn't know how long we would be gone, but I could give her Reiki every day and her wrist would heal just as well while we traveled.

I agreed to go with her and enjoyed the trip very much. As we sat side by side on the airplane, I held her wrist in the cast; so she had the Reiki every day as we went to all these places. Each day the pain was less and less and she felt more comfortable.

As we came back through Japan I asked for a bonus—that she stop at the hospital in Tokyo and have the doctors check her wrist. If it was healed I would stay and visit my teacher's family. The X-ray showed it was completely well, and when the cast was removed, she had no trouble moving her wrist and hand; so I stayed in Japan a whole month and that was the bonus I earned.

Shingles

Shingles is one of the most painful illnesses for it affects the nerves. One lady with shingles was told by the doctor it would stay a long time, sometimes years. She decided to have Reiki treatments every day, and after a month the pain was about half gone. It was not like the stinging pain at the beginning and she was getting more and more comfortable. After two months all the pain was gone, and by this time she had taken the lessons and could do it for herself. She kept on treating it every day because the numbness was still evident, and with Reiki even this slowly left her body and she was completely well. With this kind of experience, I can say that shingles can be helped and there is no need to be so crippled from it.

Because of the time and expense involved, for these long term cases it is much better for the patient and perhaps the family, too, to take the lessons and learn to do this for themselves. Reiki is the best investment a person can make for their health, for it is everlasting and can be used also for the health of everyone around them.

Kidneys

I had a call one day regarding a man on another island who was in critical condition, suffering from kidney trouble. He had moved his family back to Hawaii from the Mainland because he was unable to continue in his profession and he wanted to be with his relatives and friends. It was a condition of long-standing and he could get no further help from medical science; so he asked if I could come to his island for a little vacation and to do Reiki. I closed my office for a few days and went to treat him. After four days he had a reaction and this was a good sign that his body was accepting Reiki. He began improving and after the seventh day he asked me to stay another week and teach lessons. He and his wife, along with many relatives and friends, took the class so they could all help heal this man, and he improved until he was well again.

Indian Medicine

One day I met an Indian Chief from the East Coast and he wanted a few treatments. He was very interested in what I was doing and questioned me about my training, saying he would accept it since I had studied in the Orient and he would like to test me sometime. He explained about the Indian healers called Medicine Men, and he wanted to find out whether I had this same energy or not. I was willing to go through this test, so he arranged for me to fly to

Los Angeles and meet the Medicine Men who came from the East Coast where they lived.

When the time was set, I was there. They arrived—five of them—and the Chief said they would sit in their room while I was to go back to my room on a different floor of this large hotel and send the energy. In that way they could tell whether I had that power or not. For this test I used the Second Degree of the Usui System of Reiki, and I sent the energy to them as I had been taught to do in distant healing. After this was completed, they said, "Yes, you have passed the test." They told me it was wonderful to know that there were others who knew the method of this healing, and they were very pleased. They gave me an Indian name, Na-do-ne, which means "Wild Flower"; and they sent me a certificate saying I was a Medicine Woman.

After this test I treated the Chief for thirty days and all his ailments disappeared, so he went home completely whole. After that, every time I went to New York or New Jersey I visited him. He appreciated Reiki and was using it with very good results.

Deafness

Reiki can help cure deafness if it is caused by nerve damage. Reiki will help regenerate new nerve tissue and the hearing can be restored as the nerves are vitalized. In one class I had a lady who wanted to help her husband's deafness. He had not heard a thing for many years, but she believed so much that she wanted to give him a daily treatment. He did not believe it would help, but he was willing to let her do this just to make her happy. After about three months she was cutting out some material one day while he sat across the room reading the newspaper. Suddenly he got very excited, saying he could hear the swish, swish of the scissors as she cut the cloth. He could hear again. She continued treating him and his hearing was completely restored.

Creativity

Reiki will help whatever talent a person has, and I have had many students who found they could do many more creative things after they began working with this energy.

A lady who was a seamstress took the lessons, and afterward she said her scissors seemed to move on their own accord; and before she knew it, she had created a brand new pattern. Instead of being a seamstress only, she decided to open a small school for girls to take sewing lessons. She put an ad in the paper, and by the time she was ready to open her school she had fifty students.

One girl wanted to play music, but she did not have enough money for lessons. She worked as a typesetter for the newspaper and used her fingers every day. She bought a secondhand piano and began playing it. She even taught herself to read notes, so without lessons, she became a very good musician.

Two other people who took Reiki became very good painters, and many children who took the lessons became honor students in school.

Ulcers

One case I treated was a man with stomach ulcers. He suffered from nausea, vomiting not only mucous, but blood with it. Whenever he tried to eat, he suffered pain from the tenderness inside his stomach.

He had been eating a soft bland diet, but after twenty-one days of Reiki treatments, he was able to eat almost anything without pain and was very happy that he did not have to undergo surgery.

Cancer

Many people with cancer came for treatment—various kinds of cancer—cancer of the breast, of the stomach, even one case of the tongue. For all types, the same procedure is used: the complete treatment is given. Start from the head, then treat all the glands on the front of the body. Turn the patient over and complete the back. Last of all, go to the affected area. If the cancer is a lump the size of a large walnut, my experience is it takes only about three weeks to dissolve.

When it is a lump in the breast, the complete treatment is given, with special emphasis on the female organs, the ovaries, the uterus. Last of all, go to the lump, the affected area, and treat the breast. Many times I have seen colored areas with this cancer—

purple, red—very painful; but when the treatment is applied, the body is cleansed of its toxins; and when the organs are vitalized, the lump begins to dissolve. In many cases there was no need for surgery.

In one case the doctor found the lump, so he arranged for the lady to come in five days for surgery to remove it from her breast. That evening she came to my studio seeking help as she was very worried and afraid of the operation. As I treated her, I did find the lump about the size of a small walnut, so I concentrated on the ovarian glands. She came every day, and on the fifth when she returned to the clinic for her appointment, the doctor could not find the lump. It was completely gone. This was a very happy event for this lady, so she and her husband joined the next Reiki class, saying they wanted to always protect their health with this preventive method.

There were cases where the woman had already had a hysterectomy, and later the breast cancer. These were much slower healing because she had lost her important organs, so the whole body had to be improved first before results were obtained.

In any case involving the breast, the first cause will usually be found in the female organs. Treat the ovaries and the uterus, as well as the thyroid and the breasts. Always improve the female organs, for that is the number one cause of any breast problem.

* * *

There was a sixty-year-old man who was in a very

serious condition with cancer of the esophagus. He was in so much pain he required injections each day to help relieve the discomfort and sedate him, so he slept most of the time. The growth in his esophagus was so large he could not swallow, so he had lost a lot of weight and was hungry all the time. He could not keep anything down, not even liquid, so the doctor gave him two weeks to live.

His wife had learned Reiki, so she decided to treat him and give him as much time as possible, in spite of the doctor's diagnosis. After three days he began to feel better, more alert, telling her he did not have pain when she treated his throat. Every time she left him, for even a few minutes, he felt the pain again; so he asked her to send the three children to take the lessons so they could provide twenty-four hour treatment for his cancer. With four practitioners in the family, the father continued his progress without pain.

As he felt better, he wanted to relieve his hunger, so they started him on clear soup, which he was able to swallow. The next week he began to eat a thin gruel, then soft rice. At the end of a month he had shown such improvement the doctor decided to stop the daily injections. The man continued improving, with no pain, so the doctor X-rayed and found the growth has shrunk.

By the end of the second month, he had progressed so well that he instructed his wife to cut every orchid in his greenhouse, almost forty, and take them to

Mrs. Takata in gratitude; and to request permission to add a dish of sashimi (raw fish) and a bottle of sake to his diet. Since this was a part of his regular diet for forty years, I agreed he could have the sashimi, but only a small cup of sake, not the full bottle.

In another sixty days he began to gain weight, and in six months he returned to his job, this man who had been given only two weeks to live.

This case showed again what my teacher had instructed: We do not give up. As long as there is breath, we should try; and if there is a recovery, give the credit to Reiki.

Leukemia

On December 7, 1941, I had a guest from Honolulu. This young woman had come to visit a friend on Hawaii, and hearing about Reiki, called for an appointment. The doctors had diagnosed her problem as leukemia, and she required a weekly blood transfusion. She had come to my studio very early that morning for her first session, but because of the attack on Pearl Harbor, she was unable to return home for two weeks. She had daily treatments during this time and had begun to improve, even though she had no transfusions. She had color in her face and was much more vibrant, with greater energy. This young lady responded very well, accepting the Reiki, so she improved rapidly. She was pleased to be able to do many more things without exhaustion and wanted to take the classes so she could treat herself.

When she returned to Honolulu her friends were so impressed with her progress that there were forty-two students waiting when I arrived to teach the lessons. When they had completed the class, her friends worked on her daily for six weeks, after which she was completely well.

* * *

With leukemia, as in every case, the complete treatment is done, and with this condition you will find heat and vibrations in the spleen area. I had a case where this man was very far gone. He had to have treatment for months, and his family took the lessons so they could help him at home. After a year he went to a specialist on the Mainland, and when the doctor examined him, he told this man he had conquered leukemia. He was now healthy and could return to work in his business.

Nose Bleeds

In one of the districts where I had lectured and was preparing to teach a class, a woman came asking that she be allowed to learn Reiki in order to help her fourteen-year-old son who suffered from severe nose bleeds. These were so alarming that the school officials would not allow the boy to participate in any of the sports, saying this condition was too dangerous.

When the lessons were completed, I was preparing to leave when the father came to tell me the son's bleeding had started that morning and his mother was unable to stop it, so he asked me to come and give a treatment at their home.

When we arrived, the boy was bleeding very, very badly through the nose. I could see this was no ordinary hemorrhage, so we propped him up and began to apply cold compresses. His mother placed her hands on his solar plexus while I worked on his nose and the nape of his neck. I realized this hemorrhage was coming from an artery, for every time the heart pumped, out it gushed. It was very scary. We treated him for forty-five minutes in these positions until the bleeding stopped completely.

The parents were very relieved, for this was the first time they had ever been able to stop it. I stayed another day, working with the mother to give the boy a complete treatment. He had a weak artery in the head which allowed the hemorrhage, so we strengthened this blood vessel. Since the pressure came from below, we treated the whole body to release the tension. With only this one treatment, he never had another nose bleed and was able to live a normal life.

Sties

A young mother in one of my Reiki classes had a year-old baby son who had been born with a sty on one eye. The doctor thought this would soon go away but, instead, it had transferred to the other eye the second week after birth. This pattern continued, so during the first year of his life, this little boy had

had fifty-two sties. He was a very unhappy baby, crying and fussing constantly.

The mother wanted to obtain help for her child and asked me to treat him. Since he was yet a baby, I thought the Reiki would work very rapidly; so in the afternoon when he was napping, I went to his crib as closely as possible without disturbing him. I worked on his eyes very gently for ten minutes, then around his forehead and ears, continuing on to the front where I treated the internal organs.

When I turned him over, he was sleeping so soundly that he did not awaken. This surprised the mother since he usually woke at the slightest noise. As I was working on his back I found the cause of his problem. His kidneys were not up to par, which caused a buildup of toxins in his system from the poor elimination. I warned the mother to be prepared with a large supply of diapers, for the reaction would begin after the Reiki treatment, and the toxins would be eliminated. For forty-five minutes I treated his kidneys, and when the child awoke from his nap, he was so happy—smiling, laughing—none of his usual crying and whining.

By the next day his mother reported the sty was shrinking, and by the third treatment it had disappeared. I told her how to continue the treatments, especially his liver and kidneys, to prevent any further sties, and that was the last one he had.

Motion Sickness

On one occasion when I traveled by boat to another island to conduct classes, I found my cabin mate already aboard, lying in her bunk. We were strangers, and she asked me to please request another stateroom because she was so seasick that her moaning and groaning all night would annoy me. I went to the bunk and said, "Lady, the boat is tied up to the pier. We are still in the harbor and you say you are seasick?" "Yes, even the thought of taking the boat makes me sick, but it is necessary that I go home, so I have no choice."

She was wearing traditional Japanese garments, a kimono with obi (sash) and a Japanese coat, lying there fully dressed. I told her, "Do not worry," but foolishly did not explain that I was able to help her. I had so much confidence in my hands that I just stuck them between her obi and her kimono, in the area of the solar plexus. When she felt my hands there, she began to scream, "Help! Help!" I was red-faced right up to the ears because I had felt her wallet tucked into the sash, so it was no wonder she was shocked, lying there so helpless, thinking a stranger was trying to rob her. I did not dare remove my hands but said, "Reiki, if you are there, hurry up and do your stuff!"

She calmed down a little, trying to figure out what I was saying; so I concentrated, closed my eyes, and said, "Reiki, hurry up, hurry up!" Within a few minutes the tension in the solar plexus began to lessen, and after a few more minutes she said, "My dear lady, you have made magic." "Do you feel better?" "Yes, all the headache and nausea are gone." She was willing for me to continue, so I gave her the complete treatment even down to her feet. At the end of the hour she was a completely different woman.

The boat began its voyage out of the harbor, but the motion had no effect upon her. When it was time for dinner to be served, she ate a light meal and then slept soundly all night, completely relaxed, without any further seasickness.

Back Pain

There was a beekeeper who lived some distance from my studio. With such a large honey farm, there were many bee-hives to lift and carry, so he developed a very painful back condition which was aggravated with this lifting. He went to a large medical clinic in Honolulu, and when the doctor had examined his back and had seen the X-rays, he said this man would need a surgery on the discs in his spine. When the doctor could not guarantee his well-being with this surgery, the beekeeper decided he was not in a hurry for such an operation and, returning from Honolulu, he sought me out.

I had just begun a new class of Reiki students and could give him time for only one treatment before he went home. He was quite pleased with this treatment, went home, and began organizing a class.

When I arrived, it was a big surprise to find thirty people ready to learn Reiki.

A few months later he invited me to visit his honey farm. I was there for five days, a very lovely experience. I gave him treatments every day, with his wife joining me in these sessions, and we found him very well. He could work all day without any pain. He told me since he had his health, he was able to work and this give him financial security. He and his wife followed the Ideals of Reiki which they had learned in the class, and they were successful and happy.

Death

In the late 1930's, as I was beginning my Reiki practice, I was up early one morning sweeping the sidewalk as I prepared for the day's appointments. My neighbor's brother drove up to her house, and as she came out to join him, she stopped to speak to me, tears in her eyes, "Mrs. Takata," she said, "I have come to ask a great favor of you. I had word my mother passed away this morning at five o'clock, and my brother has come to take me home. This has been a very great shock because I did not think she was so sick. She had the flu and a fever, but it did not seem serious, so I am conscience-stricken to think that I was neglectful. If you would go with me for moral support, perhaps I will have the strength to face this sorrow." "Of course, I will go with you if it will make you feel better."

In the hour it took to drive to her parents' home,

this lady cried, feeling so badly that she had not done more for her mother, repenting her lack of concern. Her brother agreed that he, too, had neglected their parents. These seemed to me to be very sincere confessions and I hoped God had ears to hear, for only He could do anything about it.

By the time we arrived at the house, there were many people there, busily preparing for the funeral, with four men carrying the coffin into the parlor. We went into the bedroom where the mother was still lying in bed. Since I had not met this family before, I felt out of place and decided the best thing to do was to get out of their way, so I got a low stool and sat by the body of the mother. As the daughter, my neighbor, knelt and began to cry and mourn, I put both my hands on the solar plexus of the corpse, not knowing what else to do. As the daughter cried, her voice got louder and louder, confessing her shortcomings and asking God's forgiveness.

It was now nine o'clock and the mother had been declared dead for four hours. As I kept my hands on the body, I closed my eyes and began to pray, being very sincere about treating with the Reiki. This was a new experience to be asked to come where a person had passed on and had no life, but that was my duty and I felt the best thing was to continue with the Reiki since there was nothing else I could do to console them.

About ten thirty, all of a sudden, I began to feel a little warmth around her navel—or was it just my imagination? I kept my hands on and prayed harder. Unexpectedly, the woman opened her eyes and, at the same time, she opened her mouth with a big sigh. I was very surprised, saying, "Can this be true?" So still holding her solar plexus, I stood up from the stool to look into her eyes. Then she blinked, as I asked very softly, "Are you awake?" She blinked her eyes again, and when she saw a stranger standing there in front of her, she gave another sigh and said, "Oh, yes. I can see you." When she said that, I sat down again and nudged the daughter, who was bent over crying. "Stop crying and wipe your tears. Very quietly come to the other side of the bed, for your mother is asleep no more. She is alive and awake."

She saw that her mother was indeed awake and was so happy. Very gently, I then said, "Call your father," so she went into the next room where the funeral preparations were going on. When the father learned what had happened, he told the people to carry the coffin away quietly, so there was no disturbance. He came into the bedroom to see his wife, who began to ask for a big bowl of noodle soup, as she was very hungry. When the soup was brought, she insisted on sitting up and feeding herself, so we knew that she was well.

We all were delighted, and I completed the Reiki treatment on the rest of her body, still astounded at the power of God.

When the son drove me home, he expressed his

deep thanks, saying he felt very obligated; so I told him, "No, you are not obligated to me. If you want to say 'thank you,' then thank Reiki, for this is God Power." He then asked if he could start lessons so that he would be able to treat his mother. With this, I went only two days more to that household to give treatments, for the son had mastered the art of healing with Reiki.

Before I concluded my visits, not wanting to say "while you were dead," I asked the mother, "When you were in the deep sleep, where were you? Do you remember what you experienced?"

She replied, "I remember clearly. When I lost consciousness, I was in a different sphere where I was being transported very swiftly through the air. I had no feelings, no aches or pains. I saw a tunnel which had a large entrance. It was a very long tunnel with a light at the far end, and that opening was so small that I wondered how I could go through it; but once I went through, I knew I would never return. I tried to decide whether I should go through or hold back, and at that time I heard my daughter's voice calling me, 'Mama, Mama.' She was so unhappy and suffering so deeply that I came back. It was such a long sleep that when I awakened, the first thing I noticed was my hunger."

This lady lived another ten years after this experience, and the amazing thing about her recovery was that it was total and perfect. She was mentally clear and not senile; her brain was not damaged. Reiki vitalized her so she had no fever, no aches, no pain. She was able to live a full and active life.

CHAPTER EIGHT

With the passing of Grand Master Takata came the close of forty-five years in the saga of Reiki. During her time Reiki was brought from East to West, and through her, it flowed like a river, a single channel deep and broad.

Mrs. Takata's story was completed, but the story of Reiki has continued in the hundreds of students and the twenty-two Masters she had taught. From these Masters she chose as her successor her granddaughter, Phyllis Lei Furumoto. Although this young woman was trained and empowered to assume the role of Grand Master, Mrs. Takata went into transition without making a formal statement of acknowledgement. From this apparent void stepped forth another Master, Barbara Weber Ray, stating herself also to be Grand Master, successor to Mrs. Takata. The river of Reiki which was a single channel in Mrs. Takata now flowed in two major streams.

Phyllis Lei Furumoto is associated with The Reiki Alliance, a group of Masters who have stated their intent to teach in the spiritual tradition of the Mikao Usui System of Reiki, drawing to them students who also use this healing art in their conscious spiritual growth. This appears to be a blend of East and West, embodying the spirit in which Mrs. Takata taught and that in which most of her Masters continue.

Barbara Weber Ray founded the American International Reiki Association which projected a westernized image of Reiki. The purposes of this group included publishing a newsletter, establishing standards for practitioners and Masters, and helping promote a broader understanding of Reiki, with membership open to all levels of Reiki students.

Some Masters have chosen to work independently, without connection to any group.

Remembering that Reiki can do only good, that it can only heal and help bring balance, that it is Universal Life Energy, then it can be seen that Reiki is not divided but simply is working in different ways to bring itself to the world. Reiki can use many channels to carry this energy, and it will draw to itself all who are open to it, those who are willing to help create balance and growth for themselves and others. Thus, each student will be attracted to the Master from whom they are to receive the contact with this Universal Energy.

Reiki is One. We are each a part of that Oneness. Be open to this possibility and Reiki will guide you to your Teacher.